Turning In Is the Only Way Out:

My Journey Back to Peace After the Tragic Death of My Only Son

Dr. Angelia Griffin

A GOSHEN PUBLISHERS BOOK   VIRGINIA

Turning In Is the Only Way Out:
My Journey Back to Peace After the Tragic Death of
My Only Son

ISBN: 978-1-7378405-1-0
Copyright ©2022 Angelia Griffin

Library of Congress Cataloging-in-Publication Data

All rights reserved solely by the author. The author guarantees all contents are original and do not infringe upon the legal rights of any other person or work. No part of this book may be reproduced, shared in a retrieval system, or transmitted in any form or by any means, electronic, mechanical, photocopying, or recording, without prior written permission of the Author or Publisher.

Published in 2022 by:

GOSHEN PUBLISHERS LLC
P.O. Box 1562
Stephens City, Virginia, USA
www.GoshenPublishers.com

Our books may be purchased in bulk for promotional, educational, or business use. For inquiries, please contact the publisher via email: Agents@GoshenPublishers.com.

First Edition 2022

Cover designed by Goshen Publishers LLC

Printed in the United States of America

This book is dedicated to

William Donald Paul, II

who made this world a better place.

Turning In Is the Only Way Out

My Journey Back to Peace After the Tragic Death of My Only Son

Dr. Angelia Griffin

Table of Contents

Acknowledgements i
Remembering William Donald Paul, II
 (aka: Will; Mr. Certified) 1
Chapter 1: Unexpected and Tragic Loss 7
Chapter 2: The Scales of Justice 21
Chapter 3: IGMA Inc 33
Chapter 4: Faith 41
Chapter 5: Forgiveness 53
Chapter 6: Family 61
Chapter 7: Friends 67
Chapter 8: Food (E.A.T.I.N.G.) 75
Chapter 9: Fiduciary Responsibility 85
Chapter 10: Finances 93
Chapter 11: Fears 101
Chapter 12: Lessons Learned 109
The Result 117
Bonus Chapter 119
Appendices 125

ACKNOWLEDGEMENTS

First, to God, who is the head of my life, all the praise, glory, and honor for who I am today as a woman, committed to being the difference I want to see in others. I know this book would not have been possible were it not for His grace and mercy. While I knew this day would come, I often thought it would have been completed sooner. But as the old saying goes, our plans are not always God's plans.

I am most appreciative of my phenomenal parents: C. B. Griffin, Jr (my deceased father, a man to most but a hero to me) and Fannie Jo Griffin, my beautiful, supportive mother and number one fan for ALWAYS believing in all my endeavors.

To my wonderful godfather, the late John Dublin Matthews, for sharing with me his recipe for a happy life: bills, pills, and the daily reading of Psalms 23, 37, 91, and 100.

The intelligent and forward-thinking father of my children, my friend and ex-husband Dr. William D. Paul, thank you for giving me two of the most amazing and important gifts of my life: my son William Donald Paul, II, and daughter Starria (Star) Alexus Paul.

I owe my amazingly authentic, attractive, and eccentric daughter, Star (my mini me), a debt of gratitude for simply loving me. She reminded me that she needed me to help her live again after the loss of her awesome brother and best friend.

ACKNOWLEDGEMENTS

To my daughter-in-love, Keta Humphrey Peterson, I can never say THANK YOU enough for giving me my third greatest life gift, Khalil Adonis Paul, my handsome grandson, who makes me feel like my son, William, is still alive.

Also, thank you to my amazing confidante friends, who have been with me since childhood and helped me to develop into the woman I am today: Belinda Carrington, my woman of wisdom (and husband Uncle Vic—godparents of Bill and Star) and Linda Jones Sellers, my ride or die (and husband Sidney, uncle and aunt of my children). Individually and collectively, you have always seen my worth, especially when I was blinded by life's biggest disappointments. I am eternally blessed to tell the world I am grateful to have two "best friends in Belinda and Linda" because you both empower me in different ways.

To my goddaughter, Shelbra Caruthers, for all you have done to help me manage my children as they have navigated through life, in addition to helping me think through my uncertainties in my quest to be a better person.

Mary P. Ford, for your unwavering friendship, inspiration, and commitment to serve as my life and spiritual coach without judgment of me and all my flaws. To my spirit-filled older brother, Prophet Marlon Griffin, for your unwavering prayers and spiritual guidance.

My younger, entrepreneurial-minded baby brother Charlie B. Griffin III, for your ability to look beyond my faults and dwell on my assets.

Also, my mentor and friend, Dr. Samuel Sanders, for all of your shared wisdom. To Bobby Hart, a true friend and man who leads by example in all endeavors. Soror Carey Jones, my favorite Delta Sigma Theta Sorority, Inc., Sister, who in my humble opinion is my true example of real "Sisterhood". Yolanda Ward Williams, my AKA friend of the pink and green family who never waivers in friendship and support of me and my family. My longtime friends, Annette Wynn, for sharing your wisdom and ability to see my worth despite my flaws.

Margaret Timmons-Smoake, for always being willing to listen, even when what I am saying may not make sense. Dr. Mary Ann Hughes-Butts, my peer mentor and friend from FLA ("Freekin" Lower Alabama, now a resident of Las Vegas, and also my Caucasian sister from another mother) who sees no color and only accepts me for who I am and aspire to be in life. Also, my phenomenal state appointed lead attorney, friend, and sorority sister Azzie Taylor, now Alabama's Deputy District Attorney (DA), for your unwavering commitment to helping me bring justice to the woman who murdered my son.

To anyone reading this book whom I may have UNINTENTIONALLY hurt while dealing with my own hurt along the healing journey to recover my piece of peace, please accept my humble apology.

Also, to my host of family and friends whom my list is too long to name. You all know who you are and the role you have played in undergirding me with prayers and encouragement, especially when I have most felt darkness was a never-ending path of confinement I have traveled for

ACKNOWLEDGEMENTS

a decade. It is because of each of you I thank God for using you individually and collectively to stand with me when our paths have crossed.

Dr. Shawn Richmond, thank you very much for taking the time to meet with me after several years of disconnect. I remember when we first met, I shared with you God had ordered me to sit at your feet and I am so grateful I was obedient then and now. I believe God used you, Dr. Richmond, to help me birth this book regarding my aspirations to complete this story, summarizing a decade of my life in bondage. I am so grateful for your untiring willingness as you personally helped me put pen to paper to ensure the completion of this book in an effort to share with the world. I sincerely appreciate the additional resources you placed at my fingertips, and the team of professionals who walk alongside you at Goshen Publishers, especially Sarah Lamb, for professionally editing my manuscript. Above all, I appreciate the time you took to pray with me and reassure me we were both following God in this endeavor.

DEAR READER:

We are each given a birthday and an expiration day. Traditionally, children are expected to bury their parents. Nowhere is it written that parents are expected to bury their children. When a parent has to bury a child, the common denominator is hurt and grief. Death is final, and grieving is a natural state of mind. How one grieves typically varies from one person to the next. Essentially, there is no one way to determine the way people grieve, as we are all unique human beings who can agree the feeling(s) resulting from the death of a loved one is complete with a host of overwhelming and uncontrollable emotions. Thus, the overall feelings and emotions associated with losing a loved one, especially a child, are very personal and become a journey to establish even a sliver of peace.

The focus of this book is to share eight essential ingredients for peace and wholeness, along with twenty-one lessons I have learned. These have helped me to overcome a feeling of bondage and confinement resulting from the unexpected and tragic murder of my only son when he was away at college. It is my humble hope after reading each chapter and completing each activity nestled at the end of each chapter in this book, you will also be in a better space to establish a greater sense of purpose, which may help lead you on your healing journey to finding resolve bigger than your pain.

Finally, to every person reading this compilation of heartfelt thoughts, it is my prayer after reading the last words on the final page of this book, you too will be **E**ncouraged, **M**otivated, and **E**mpowered (EME) to continue living a refreshed life in a world where you really do matter despite life's disappointments.

Prayerfully,
Dr. A.

Remembering William Donald Paul, II

(aka: Will; Mr. Certified)

Giving birth to a child is a blessing from God. I was blessed twice. As a parent, perhaps one may agree that because as no instructions are given after birth, the whole idea of parenting rests on choices. Upon becoming a parent, the first step is to provide a place of shelter for your child, followed by establishing a process to help your child to grow up and become a healthy, law-abiding citizen.

There are high and low points, which all parents experience in raising children. In my opinion, little girls have, and require, different needs from those of little boys, and I am grateful, proud, and honored to be a mother of two completely opposite children. For instance, William, (also called Will or Bill throughout these pages) became my full-of-life and fun-loving child, whereas my amazing, eccentric, one-of-a-kind daughter Star is a daddy's girl who is quite the opposite of her brother. I love both of my phenomenal children; however, I strongly believe there is nothing like a mother's love for her son.

Spending quality time with my son throughout his life created a strong bond, in which William deputized himself as my protector at a very young age. Often, I recall when my son would say, "I am the man of the house." Although my children have an amazing father, I must publicly admit, in my early twenties, I was too immature to recognize how blessed our children were to have a real father in their lives from birth.

Unfortunately, later I divorced my children's dad with no thought of what their lives might have been like in the future had I not been a self-centered wife and young woman trying to find myself during the early years of marriage. Truthfully, I made several uninformed choices for which I am not overly proud. Nevertheless, my children's father and I have remained true friends over the past three plus decades, namely because we promised never to divorce our children despite ending our six-year marriage.

Raising William and Star was achieved through co-parenting and through the help of a host of family and friends. Our children never had a need that was not met by one, if not both, parents. Our children were five years apart, with a genuine sibling love for one another. Although Star never experienced living in the home with both her father and me, our son spent his first few years in the world under the roof of both parents. It is safe to say our son provided both of his parents with a major sense of accomplishment.

When William became a teenager, he asked as a Christmas wish to be granted the privilege to move to Montgomery, Alabama, to live with his father. I had no reservations about agreeing. In my heart, I thought I had done all I could do to help our son become a teenager. I recall thinking to myself, who best to help our son become a man than his father?

The move to Montgomery positioned William to experience southern living in the ever-evolving state of

Alabama. After a few years, and developing into a fine young man who excelled in most endeavors and was well loved by family, friends, and acquaintances, William earned his high school diploma at Wetumpka High School. Later, he became an aspiring student at Alabama State University, where he became a young father and coparent to our amazing grandson, Khalil Adonis Paul, whom he loved with a passion.

THAT IS WHERE THIS STORY BEGINS.

Chapter 1: Unexpected and Tragic Loss

My life was good. I was healthy, gainfully employed, productive, and happy. I had friends, a social life, a loving family, and for the most part, all was well. That changed forever when I received that one phone call. It informed me that my son had been shot. He was away at college attempting to stop two women from fighting off campus. Within minutes from the time I received the call, William was pronounced dead on the scene. He was gone.

In an effort to share the account of my nightmare of losing William, I decided to broaden my understanding of the topic of gun violence. Statistics show that more than 100 Americans are killed by guns and more than 230 are shot and wounded every day.[1] The effects of gun violence in America extends far beyond these casualties—it shapes the lives of millions of Americans who witness it, know someone who was shot, or even live in fear of the next shooting. Those victims have families, friends, and communities that are impacted. None of their lives are ever the same.

Everytown Research recorded that "58 percent of American adults or someone they care for have experienced gun violence in their lifetime." The data shows that gun violence is on the rise no matter where we work, live, or

---

[1] Data retrieved from *Everytown Research,*
https://everytownresearch.org/report/gun-violence-in-america/

Chapter 1: Unexpected and Tragic Loss

play. Based on these alarming facts, I want to encourage you to proceed with reading the remaining pages of this book by first asking yourself three simple questions:

- ➤ Have you tragically lost a loved one whose death came to you as a total bombshell?

- ➤ Are you at a point in your life where you are able to share details comfortably regarding how your loved one died?

- ➤ Can you reflect and honestly communicate your overall feelings regarding your loss?

Now, before you put pen to paper, allow me to invite you to follow me on my healing journey. After years of bondage and confinement, it has taken me to a place of freedom and wholeness. As you are reading my story, you will also have opportunities to provide and record responses to questions at the end of each chapter. In like manner, at the end of this book, you may choose to connect with me to help you take the next step toward your place of holistic peace, should you desire to use my story as a place of reference.

Sometimes bad things happen to good people. This was the case of my son, William Donald Paul II (affectionately known to many of his college peers and acquaintances as "Mr. Certified"). At the age of twenty-four, he was attempting to stop two off-campus young women from fighting. One of the women was Williams's friend. The other woman lived in a nearby complex where Will had borrowed a car jack from a resident. He did not know this resident. His intent was to remove the rims from his ex-girlfriend's car

Chapter 1: Unexpected and Tragic Loss

because he had purchased them when they were in a relationship. The woman who pulled the trigger was the significant other of the person whom my son had borrowed the $19.99 car jack from. William's current girlfriend got into an altercation with that woman. My son was trying to break them up.

At the time of the incident, William was in preparation for his junior year of enrollment at Alabama State University (ASU). Mr. Certified was the name coined by William and a host of male followers. William had told them that they each needed to obtain a high school diploma, GED, attend college, and/or go into the military in order to be considered as one of his close friends and certified. He became affectionately known in the community where he worked, played, and attended college as "Mr. Certified". It was written on all his custom painted cars and admired and remembered by his peers.

The date was December 2, 2010. Earlier in the day, I felt led to call William and tell him he had been in my spirit heavily all day. I knew I had to stop what I was doing and call to pray with him at that moment, as everywhere I turned throughout the day, I could see his face.

He said, "Yes, Mama, 'cause you know I don't ever want to disrespect you."

I then restated the question, and I asked my son if I could pray with him right then.

He agreed, not knowing this would be our last conversation. He stopped all his movement and listened to me pray for and with him, and he concluded with an "Amen".

My eyes tear now as I recall how my last conversation with my one and only son ended with prayer. I had told him, "I do not know what you are going through right now, but I need to pray with you right now!" As I prayed with him, I said, "God is bigger than whatever you are going through. God loves you and so do I!"

Shortly after I hung up the phone, I received a call from the young lady he was dating. She was screaming, "Will has been shot!"

I was driving to teach my class at the University of Phoenix (UoP). I immediately called William's phone. Thank God, one of William's close friends, Houston, answered his phone. He confirmed what the girlfriend had said.

I screamed, "Tell me what is happening."

Houston kept crying and saying, "I just know Will has been shot."

I could hear sirens, yelling, screaming, and talking among the onlookers. I knew it was not good. With my heart racing, I yelled, "Tell me what is happening."

Houston said in distress, "I don't know what all happened yet!"

I pleaded, "Please tell the police it's his mama on the phone."

CHAPTER 1: UNEXPECTED AND TRAGIC LOSS

He did just as I requested and shouted to the police officer who had arrived on the scene, "It's Dr. Mama, Will's mama, on the phone."

I was still driving, but I am not sure now how I managed to. Through my phone headset, I could hear the officer's response. "It's a crime scene and I can't talk to her right now."

I yelled back, "Ask him to PLEASE talk to me", all the while knowing the situation was grave.

Again, I was told, "He can't talk to you right now!"

I asked Houston to just put the phone down in the middle of the area so I could hear what was going on. I also requested, "Please come back to the phone as soon as possible to tell me how William is doing."

It was several minutes before Houston came back to the phone to give me an update, but it felt like an eternity. To my surprise, no one moved the phone from the crime scene, so I could still hear all the background noises. I was driving to UoP, to teach the final night of my course. I continued to glance at my phone and pray. Time seemed to stand still as I cried out to God, begging Him to save my son. The clock in my Navigator showed a little over thirty-five minutes had elapsed from the time I received the call.

To say the least, I felt totally helpless. I was in a different state, so I could not rush to his side. I had no details, so I could not solicit help. I had love and I had prayer. The tears flowed down my cheeks as if someone had poured a pitcher of water from the top of my head and down the front of my face. My heart raced with each second that passed.

I prayed for God to cover my son with His unconditional love. I thought about calling my mom and asking her to pray because I remembered her prayers seemed to get a quicker response from God. Yet, I did not because I was so afraid I would cause the call to drop.

I continued to drive at a snail's pace because I was stuck in rush hour traffic. I did not call the school to tell anyone what was going on, again, because I worried it might accidentally disconnect the call. I stayed on that call as I continued to drive through the relentless Atlanta traffic and across the infamous "Spaghetti Junction" to Gwinnett. I cried. I prayed. I drove. I waited. I listened. I hoped.

The traffic was so hectic, I felt like I was in a parking lot where all the vehicles were moving at an inch at a time. I knew I could not get off the highway because exiting would have only compounded my situation. I called out to Jesus. I prayed that my son would live.

Houston finally picked up the cell phone. He said that he could still see William.

I responded with a rapid series of questions, "How is he doing? What is going on? How is he looking?"

Houston said solemnly, "Dr. Mama, he is not looking good because he is losing a lot of blood."

Chapter 1: Unexpected and Tragic Loss

A minute or so went by. I could hear Houston's heavy breathing and the murmuring from onlookers. William's friend sounded like he was crying.

In a loud, weeping voice, I said, "Tell me what is going on."

"Dr. Mama, they are pulling the white sheet over him."

"No!" I cried out even louder, screaming "NO, NO, NO, NO, NO!"

Together, Houston and I cried.

I could hear the police telling everyone to get back, and then the phone went silent.

To this day, I am confident William lived approximately thirty-five minutes after he was shot, based on the length of that phone call.'

Later, during the grand jury murder trial, I learned that my son lived long enough to tell the officer on the scene and point directly to the person who shot him. She was a known neighborhood bully who lived in a nearby housing complex.

A short time later, I called the school and shared what had happened. Then, I called my then husband, immediately followed by calls to William's father, and my mom. Afterwards, I called my confidante and the children's godmother, Belinda, followed by my other confidante, Linda, to share the bad news and asked Linda to check on my mom, who was alone when I called.

Chapter 1: Unexpected and Tragic Loss

I remember being asked where I was and if I would allow someone to come and pick me up. I was in shock. I could not believe it was not all a horrible dream. I told everyone I was headed to the school because the traffic was too bad to turn around and head home. As expected, they were all worried about me.

When I arrived at work with tears streaming down my face, I was greeted by the staff and a classroom full of silent students. For the most part, everyone was quiet until I uttered, "I am okay."

I reminded everyone that the traffic was horrible, and we should all simply continue with completing the class expectations, seeing how this was the last night of class and final oral presentations were due. God's grace and mercy shielded my mind to a place where I was able to exist and cope in the face of adversity.

Thankfully, for the last night of class, I had already scheduled a guest speaker to arrive and share with the learners how to apply their skills to propel them into their respective careers. The speaker was a person I had recently met; however, she facilitated the class in a manner that suggested we had planned strategically how the class would end, although we had not. Ironically, throughout the five weeks of knowledge sharing, I had constantly reminded the amazing group of valued adult learners that managers and real leaders had to always be ready to rise above, regardless of life's obstacles.

At the end of the class, I must admit I simply hated watching the students drive off because I realized I was

Chapter 1: Unexpected and Tragic Loss

really alone and I had an hour's commute back to my residence in Powder Springs, Georgia. Several students and staff hung around to make sure I would be okay. I reassured them I was fine, when in fact, I could not wait to get back in my car and pull off the false mask I'd been wearing which suggested I was fine.

There was one student, a young man, whom I noticed early in the class looked like my son. I looked at this young man with tears rolling down my cheeks. He had tears in his eyes, and I reminded the student I appreciated him being in my class. The learner thanked me for what he felt was the best class experience he had encountered in the entire program in pursuit of his undergraduate business degree.

Truthfully, I thought at the end of my class the student would have complained in my end of course survey about how hard I pushed him to overcome his fear of public speaking. To my surprise, and that of the student's peers, this learner had improved so much from the first night the class started. The students and I agreed, had there been a Most Improved Professional Student Award, without a doubt, this young man would have been the recipient.

I share this memory because this young man looked so much like my son, that I felt for a moment my situation was merely a dream. When the student drove off from the campus, I hurried to my car and slumped over my steering wheel, reflecting on the dreadful reality that my son was gone. The tears poured down my face again. My heart hurt.

After a while, I started my car and headed home. The traffic was still heavy, but not quite as bad as it was during my commute to work. I checked back in with my family to let them know I was en route. My heart was beating fast, and my head was so heavy throughout my drive, but thank God, I made it home safely. I do not remember who I saw first because there was a crowd when I arrived. By the time I walked in, someone was saying, "Sit down, breathe, and try to relax."

Sitting down was easier than breathing and relaxing. I think my reality set in when I saw Williams's dad and his wife. She's a medical doctor and prescribed a valium to help me relax and try to rest. I did not sleep for days. While sitting in my living room with tears streaming down my face, I recall Shelbra, my mentee and daughter from another mother, answering a host of phone calls and taking messages, because as one can imagine, I was in no shape to talk to anyone.

During those first few days, mostly, I recall my head and my heart throbbing as if they were competing with one another. I do not recall eating a morsel of food for several days, which is a true telling sign I was in distress because eating is my favorite hobby.

After a few days, I came to my senses. I had to plan. Although I had people offering to help, I knew the bond I shared with Will, and I could not pass this duty off to just anyone. So, four or five days after the tragedy, I felt I was ready to plan my son's funeral.

Earlier in the year, I had experienced a premonition. It was almost like a dream, showing me that something bad was going to happen to one of my children. I simply did not know which child would be affected. I remember going back to sleep after several short dreams, only to awaken and realize I was experiencing the same awful dream. One day, I called my mom and shared my dream as best I could recall. She was speechless when I shared with her the details.

The dream was so real that several times throughout the same year I attempted to establish a life insurance policy on my children, but the process became difficult because my son was away at college in Montgomery, Alabama, and my daughter was away at college in Statesboro, Georgia. When my son's death happened, financially, I did not have my affairs in order as I had hoped.

Time passed by swiftly when I had to make what I believe was the hardest decision regarding Will's burial. Funding was very, very, very tight, but God sent help. While preparing for the funeral, a few friends shared knowledge and resources to help bury William with the basic expectations having been met. My family and I were blessed to have a memorial service on Wednesday, December 8, 2010, at 6:30 p.m. at the Good Hope Missionary Baptist Church, located in Wetumpka, Alabama. The seating was at capacity with standing room only. William's schoolmates, friends, co-workers, church members, and onlookers filled the building. The presiding Bishop presented William's father and me with an honorary bachelor's degree from the New Covenant International Bible College. He did so in memory of William's ability to bring and lead young men to the church to gain an understanding of the Bible.

CHAPTER 1: UNEXPECTED AND TRAGIC LOSS

Several people spoke at the memorial service, including William's pastor, his girlfriend, and a young man from the community where William had started a nonprofit group called SQUASHIT. That is where he helped to encourage young black boys to set goals and strive to achieve more out of life than they were accustomed to seeing. While I do not remember all the details of the memorial service, I remember two powerful moments.

First, a young man was dressed in an outdated, all-white outfit called a "Love Boned" suit, which made him look like he was going to perform with the Temptations at a concert. He shared he was dressed that way because, "Will had always taught us, the kids from the neighborhood project, to dress up for something in life." He felt the need to dress up for Will on the night of the memorial.

The same young man also told a story about a time when Will and his father arranged to bring in athletes from Atlanta to speak and motivate the boys to be all they could be and not fight each other. Will had planned a fundraiser to wash cars for the purpose of raising money to help pay for the pizzas they would eat when the athletes came.

On that day, Will handed him a $100.00 bill and instructed him to go inside the store and purchase the supplies they needed for the car wash fundraiser. He said he was both surprised and thankful because Will had placed in his hand more money than he had ever received in his life without it being drug related.

The young man and his heartfelt comments inspired me to speak on behalf of my son. William always looked for

CHAPTER 1: UNEXPECTED AND TRAGIC LOSS

ways to bring youth together, although he himself was constantly being stopped by the police for playing his music very loud.

Another memorable moment was listening to William's pastor speak, who said, "William was always coming into church with a group of young men. He instructed the young men to sit in the middle of the sanctuary because he said his mama never permitted him and his sister to sit in the back of the church because trouble was too easy to get into." After many church services, the pastor said William would always encourage him to speak to one, if not all, of the young men with positive and encouraging words. He finished with, "I wish there were more like William Paul in the church, because I feel the world would be a better place!"

When William's pastor stopped talking, I rose from my seat and walked to the microphone to speak. I had overheard a number of the young people chanting that they wanted to kill the woman who killed Will. I do not recall everything I said, but I do remember challenging the young people in the audience to remember William was not about violence. In many Christian church services, there is what is called an "altar call". That's an opportunity for people to convert or to receive special prayer. When the altar call was made, I observed more than fifty young people making their way down to the altar for prayer or to accept Jesus Christ in their respective lives.

While I miss William tremendously, I said then and I still believe now, "I would rather have William spend his life with

Jesus than in jail." You see, I believe if William had not been murdered on that day, he may have attempted to retaliate had his friend been shot instead of him.

Immediately after the memorial in Alabama, my family, friends, and I traveled back to Georgia to prepare for the final homegoing service for William. The funeral service was held Thursday, December 9, 2010, at 2:00 p.m. at my home church, Destiny World Church, in Austell, Georgia under the leadership of our Senior Pastor Wilbur T. Purvis, III. My older brother Prophet Marlon Griffin delivered a very uplifting sermon.

A few years before William's death, my brother had eulogized my father. William asked my brother to deliver his eulogy if he went home to be with the Lord before he did.

During his sermon for William, Prophet Griffin walked the attendees of the homegoing service through the alphabet (A-Z) of the Bible. His stepdaughter and my niece, Erica Griffin, sang, "He Wants It All". Erica's angelic voice blessed my soul beyond words. When the committal service was complete and the lowering of the casket occurred, I remember saying to myself, "I can't breathe". It felt like the weight of the world was on my chest.

William was well loved and now royally missed by so many who traveled from near and far to bear witness to his homegoing service. At the end of the service, I realized I was angry. I was so angry that I did not want to continue living. That is why I allowed myself to enter into a place of confinement and bondage.

Chapter 2: The Scales of Justice

Although I continued to live above ground, my inner spirit checked out. I pretended like I was okay, though I was not. I tried to remain busy so I would not have to face the world in the state of mind I was in.

For the next year and a half, I remember driving back and forth from Powder Springs, Georgia, to Montgomery, Alabama, countless times to prepare for the grand jury murder trial. I recall sitting in the courtroom one bench behind the heartless murderer of my beloved son. I am not violent, but at that moment I wanted to hit her, to punch that woman in her face. Of course, I knew that would have only made me feel good momentarily, but also, quite possibly, could have landed me in jail with her. With that thought, I also reminded myself that I do not look good in orange.

Sitting there, I remained calm and somewhat composed until the judge called my name and asked if I knew the case was proceeding to the grand jury. I stood up and acknowledged her comments. Truthfully, I was confused at what that meant and simply replied, "Okay".

As I left the courtroom, I noticed the shooter standing in the breezeway, signing some documents. I was angry and grieving. I somehow remained composed as I walked right up to her, the woman who had taken my son from me, and told her, "I forgive you."

Chapter 2: The Scales of Justice

She looked at me as if she had seen a ghost, and responded, "You have no idea what you just did for me."

I did not respond, although I heard her attorney ask, "Who was that woman?" and she replied, "I think that was his mother".

We went our separate ways. My daughter Star, and daughter-in-love Keta Humphrey Peterson, and mother of my grandson, followed me out of the courtroom, letting me know they had my back and were ready to back me up if I wanted to take her out. They, too, were angry and grieving. We were all still feeling an extreme level of pain over the loss of our William.

In the months to come, our family endured weeks of sad testimonies presented by both the prosecutor and the defense team. We sat through twelve of the 911 calls that confirmed the shooter was a neighborhood adult bully. Not one of the 911 callers was willing to share their name because each was afraid she or her family might retaliate. During the trial, my family and I had to always be escorted, even to the restroom, to keep us safe during the trial.

Sadly, the first trial ended in a hung jury, during which time the judge asked my amazing team of state appointed attorneys and me to approach the bench. The judge advised me that he'd placed me on the team with my attorneys because he felt I had enough professional and academic credentials to share in making all final decisions for my son. However, he explained he felt the probability of getting all twelve jurors to agree on a verdict of murder or manslaughter was not probable.

Chapter 2: The Scales of Justice

The judge told me that I had to make a decision to accept the prosecutor's plea or move forward with a second trial. I asked what my options were, and was told I had the choice of stopping further proceedings and allowing him, as the presiding judge, to decide what the final ruling would be or agree to schedule a retrial. Being passionate and dedicated to the justice my son deserved, I opted to schedule a retrial.

The first trial ended in a hung jury because not all the jurors could unanimously agree on the final verdict. The retrial lasted for approximately two weeks. During the second trial, the defense attorney did not put the shooter back on the stand. Thankfully, the jurors deliberated less than three hours in the second trial to arrive at a guilty verdict of manslaughter. In the state of Alabama, murder and manslaughter, although closely related, their definitions and penalties differ. There are no degrees of murder in Alabama. Murder is a type of homicide that requires intent. In the case of a murder, a person would need to have a reasonable period of time to reflect on the potential consequences of their actions and still voluntarily choose to carry those actions out, and those actions result in the death of another. The Code of Alabama §13A-6-2 defines murder as the intentional death of another due to "extreme indifference to human life" or during the commission of certain crimes that result in the death of another person. The major difference between manslaughter and murder is that manslaughter does not require intent. In other words, those charged with manslaughter generally do not have the required premeditated intent to cause a person's death, even though a person's death may result from their actions. There are

Chapter 2: The Scales of Justice

usually two types of manslaughter in most states: voluntary and involuntary. Manslaughter is defined in the Code of Alabama §13A-6-3 as when a person:

> *Recklessly causes the death of another person, or causes the death of another person under circumstances that would constitute murder §13A-6-2; except that he causes the death due to a sudden heat of passion caused by provocation recognized by law, and before a reasonable time for passion to cool and for reason to reassert itself.*

Nonetheless, once I heard the verdict shared by the Juror's Foreperson, which was restated and accepted by the judge, immediately, I quickly exited the courtroom running behind the head juror, the foreperson. When I caught up with the foreperson, I was out of breath, but managed to ask, "How were you and the rest of the jurors able to return a guilty verdict in such a short duration of time?"

The foreperson replied, "Who are you?"

Once I explained William was my son, the foreperson shared his condolences and told me he served as a local minister and agreed with the other jurors that the case was clear cut. The woman who pulled the trigger was guilty as charged, based on the evidence presented during the trial. Our conversation was not long, but was very informative in helping me to understand what had just transpired in the

Chapter 2: The Scales of Justice

courtroom. At the end of our conversation, I made my way back up to the courtroom to join my family. By then, the shooter was being handcuffed to return to lockup, although she had been out on bond for several months. The judge advised we would return to his courtroom in a couple of weeks for the final sentencing.

For the weeks leading up to the second trial, I encouraged family, friends, and acquaintances to write letters about my son's character and mail them to the courts to help ensure the judge had a clear picture of the positive character he demonstrated academically, professionally, and socially. Thankfully, many people did express their views on William's behalf. During the final sentencing, the judge agreed that the shooter had single handedly and negatively impacted the life and loved ones of William forever. He also pointed out a few facts during the sentencing:

- During both grand jury trials, she displayed no remorse for her actions nor to the family, considering William's mother sat just a few feet away from her when she took the stand.

- She demonstrated no thought for human life outside of hers, even though she also was a mother and a caregiver at the time of the fatal incident.

- The action was not in self-defense, as she claimed her police training taught her to defuse the situation she basically inserted herself into at the time of the incident.

Chapter 2: The Scales of Justice

"Will has been shot!" These words ring out like a broken record for me every year on December 2. By now, one would think the memories of that dreadful day would have subsided, but they have not. I still hurt. I still get sad. I still visit the cemetery almost weekly. I still cannot believe my one and only son was snatched at the height of becoming an awesome man, father, brother, grandson, cousin, uncle, and friend. William had a bright promising future, and one might have agreed at the time of the fatal shot to his chest, everyone loved him except for the one person, who without regard for human life, took it upon herself to pull the trigger on an unarmed black male.

Both my son's godmother and I were given the opportunity to speak at the final hearing. Neither of us were permitted to face or look the shooter in the eyes. We had to face the judge while she was forced to stand beside us and listen to what we each had to say. Speaking from my heart while trying to fight back the bucket of tears that streamed down my face, now I cannot remember most of what I said. On the other hand, William's godmother proceeded to share her personal, heartfelt response. Belinda admitted she was speaking off the cuff. She also shared that she saw the shooter with her Bible during the trial and Belinda reminded her until the words in the Bible found their way from the book into her heart, they were just words on the pages.

Belinda also reminded her that she had prayed that morning not just for us, but also for the shooter's family, who did not have a say in the matter. After Belinda asked God for his guidance on what to say, the two words which

Chapter 2: The Scales of Justice

God gave her were remorse and compassion, which she shared in her response. The shooter had made a big deal on the witness stand about having gone through police academy training, where she mentioned she was taught to control the situation like the one she found herself in. Belinda reminded the judge that the shooter also said she had learned the importance of using the least amount of force necessary to gain control of the situation to deescalate rather than escalate the situation. Why was that control not used?

Belinda also has to relive this incident each year because the murder occurred the day before her 50th birthday. Often, Belinda has reminded me that the scale of justice is not always equal. Thus, she has continued to repeat time and time again, as was instilled in her by her grandmother, "Lord, don't move the mountain, but give me the strength to climb."

After Belinda and I spoke before the judge, the killer was provided an opportunity to speak to us. For the first time during the entire trial, we heard a sarcastic, "I'm sorry", as she tilted her head toward me. In my opinion, that woman shared no heartfelt emotions. She sounded as if someone made her say those words during the final sentencing. Nonetheless, the judge reminded her she was the main reason he was sentencing her to the maximum allotted time for her crime of manslaughter.

On May 24, 2012, Kandi A. Johnson received a sentence of twenty years in prison for the manslaughter of William Donald Paul II on December 2, 2010. As of the writing of this book, after having only served seven years of her twenty-year sentence, she is up for parole. My desire is that she will never be released because her actions were absolutely senseless. I do not want the perpetrator to be released back into society, mainly because I believe when a person commits a crime without true self-defense, there is also reason to secure that person. Further, the person should serve their designated sentence for the criminal behavior by which they have been convicted by a unanimous set of jurors reflective of their peers.

The perpetrator admitted she took matters into her own hands. She tried to justify it by stating during the initial trial, "All my life I had to fight." That statement affirmed her position as a neighborhood bully. My son was unarmed when he tried to break up the shooter and his girlfriend during that altercation. William never put his hands on the woman, yet she demonstrated her full disregard for human life when she pulled the trigger of the gun in the apartment complex parking lot that day.

With every bone and muscle in my body, I have campaigned very hard to keep her behind bars. As I pray daily and travel to the beach every Sunday, I ask God to search my heart and please do not let me make this hurdle in my life a malicious decision. I have sent out emails, posted social media notifications, and asked others to join me in writing to the Alabama Pardons and Parole Board. However, I have not told people what to write; I simply asked them to share their heartfelt views, hoping together we could make sure that woman remains behind bars for

Chapter 2: The Scales of Justice

the senseless killing of my son the full duration of her twenty-year sentence.

Dealing with my son's death has come with a set of challenges, including having to relive his death all over again. I felt as if someone had pulled back the scab of my deepest wound and caused the original pain to start all over again. My attorney, Azzie Taylor, asked me to share the letter which I wrote from my heart (see Appendix 3) to the courts so she could read it at the hearing. My letter was supported by additional letters (see Appendix 3) from my daughter Star, my grandson's mother Keta Humphrey Peterson, and his godmother Belinda Carrington (see Appendix 3).

When I received a response to my letter from the Alabama Bureau of Pardons and Paroles, confirming receipt of my letter of opposition (see Appendix 3), I experienced a sigh of relief. There was justice for William.

William is gone and the person who killed him can still see and write to her family and friends, but she is still incarcerated and serving her sentence.

Amid all the other obstacles we face in this ever-changing society, and amid a pandemic, senseless gun violence is one of my main struggles to understand. I am convinced the struggle is real and the struggle is truly not over.

However, this book is not about me, as I simply need to serve and remind guardians, God has not forgotten us. God is still with us and our children whose lives were snatched

Chapter 2: The Scales of Justice

unexpectedly. I believe only the devil comes to steal, kill, and destroy (John 10:10). Therefore, as a believer in Christ Jesus, my son is waiting to see and embrace me again.

I strive to continue forward and share that within this book, know I am still a mom who hurts deeply and mourns often over the loss of my amazing son. At the same time, my pain continues to subside because I experienced a moment late in my journey, where I could emphatically say: "I get it!" I believe in God's 4 Ps for all believers: Plan, Purpose, Promise, and Provision. The life we all live must include helping others despite our circumstances.

To my surprise, I have found myself praying for my son's killer more often than I care to admit because although what she did when she slayed my son was wrong, I am not God. I do not have a heaven or hell to put her in. So, I have been preparing myself for the day God reveals to me it is time for her to be mainstreamed back into society. I continue to solicit prayers from God Almighty because I cannot bring my son back. I do not like the idea of his slaughterer being able to freely walk around, especially when his son keeps experiencing major milestones and says things like, "I wish my dad were here".

It is my hope the remainder of this book will inspire and empower those who are attempting to navigate their new normal without a loved one, and will find peace as a result of reading my healing journey to date. So, buckle up and prepare to walk a mile with me on my journey of *Turning In!*

Despite life's tragedy of losing my one and only son and feeling like a prisoner sleeping in my own emotions called

Chapter 2: The Scales of Justice

bondage, I will always believe a love between a mother and her son is special and worth documenting to share with others.

> *"One day, we are all going to depart this place we call society, the real questions are when, where, and how?"*

CHAPTER 2: THE SCALES OF JUSTICE

TURNING IN

Where am I in my thoughts about my loss today?

What did I take from this chapter as I turn inward and reflect?

What have I done, or can I start doing to turn my tragedy into triumph?

Chapter 3: IGMA Inc

Most people have experienced some kind of pain or passion about something or someone. Pain is often a lingering experience of hurt, whereas passion often entails a desire to share or bring an awareness to a personal concern for which one maintains others may also have or be experiencing, simply being a little less vocal about. In my case, I now use my pain and passion from having lost my son as a driving force, which fuels my desire to empower others.

In memory of William, whom I feel is looking down on all those who partner with me to ensure he is never forgotten, and along with the help of a few of my dearest friends, I Give Myself Away (IGMA) was established. IGMA is a nonprofit 501(c)(3) organization, committed to a humanitarian approach as a result of my/our loss. We strive to align the efforts of IGMA with other individuals and organizations to make a positive difference in the community and help people with their coping skills. More specifically, we endeavor to collaborate in order to help bring awareness and solutions to the problems that plague our diverse society, especially those of our teens and young adults in our service areas. We strongly believe we must pool our efforts with others to stop violence and make a positive difference in the community where many teens and young adults attend school, live, work, and play.

For me personally, I am a servant leader, higher learning adjunct professor, entrepreneur, consultant, and above all servant of God, committed to reaching out to others to support and join forces with IGMA in order that we may turn a tragedy into triumph. As the founder and Chief Executive Officer (CEO) of IGMA, I am committed to making a positive difference in the community specializing in *"empowering others through training, developing, and hosting community awareness initiatives to enhance individual and organizational coping skills"*.

IGMA relies mostly on the continuous generosity of others in our efforts to present our Annual Certified Good Deeds Educational Scholarship in Memory of William Donald Paul II to deserving recipients. My goal is never to take a salary from the organization, but rather relying on our organization to cover any company expenses associated with achieving our organization's goals and objectives. Officers agree to pool their efforts as we strive to carry out the mission and vision of our organization.

A short while after my son's death, I spoke with our board of directors about bringing awareness to the concept of bullying. Often, people think of bullying as the bad behavior that typically only happens between children. Unfortunately, bullying also bleeds over into adulthood. People who are bullies as a child often grow up to bully people as an adult.

To show the link between the negative impacts of bullying and the increasing death rate in society, IGMA hosted its first stage play, *I Give Myself Away*, under the direction of Denise James, a phenomenal playwright. The plot showed the impacts of bullying and how our society is plagued by its mere existence. Local and talented youth showcased their amazing talents, depicting how bullying, coupled with gun violence, is negatively impacting our communities.

We are blessed to have many helping us with the mission of IGMA, and in multiple ways. ShaToria "Tori" Carrington was instrumental in creating our original logo, based on what I had seen in a dream—a set of hands helping others. After brief conversations with Belinda and Tori, it was almost as if God took our words and placed the image in Tori's brain to create the logo. I cannot thank Tori enough for her ability to see the vision and draw it to perfection. We have never altered our original logo, which I am confident has become our true brand, signifying what we do at IGMA.

My grandson also was instrumental in me wanting to keep my son's legacy alive. One day we stopped by his dad's grave site to fellowship and hang out at the place where he last had an encounter with his dad's body. I felt a strong desire to do something in memory of my son, but I just did not have a clear idea as to which way to turn because I was still deep in my grief. While visiting I begin to cry, just like all the other times I had stopped by to feel close to my son. On this particular day, my grandson grabbed me with both hands pressed up against my cheeks. While looking me straight in my eyes he said, "Grandma Angelia, you got to stop all this crying 'cause my daddy is not dead, He is just asleep with Jesus".

Now, as I reflect on that moment, I am confident God used my grandson to help steer me into a higher place on my healing journey. This was the day I began to realize I had to do something to keep my son's legacy alive. So, I yielded to the strong tug on my heart to put actions behind the idea of creating a nonprofit to help bring awareness to "bullying" which I believe was the underlying factor regarding how my son was murdered, in hopes of preventing anyone else from having to experience my pain.

Sharing how our nonprofit was established was key to my healing. At the time when I was driving home after visiting my son's grave site, I remember the Lord telling me to leverage all my personal and professional experiences to start our nonprofit. At first, I did not know what to name the organization. After several visits to the cemetery where William is buried, I was listening to the song "I Give Myself Away" by William McDonald. I thought to myself, what is the significance behind this song playing every time I drove William's yellow Dodge Magnum? Finally, the Lord's voice appeared in my thoughts and said, "Pull over and write down the first letter of each word of the song".

Without any hesitation I did, and the name of IGMA was established. Shortly after, I reached out to Dr. Paul and those who would essentially become our original officers. I wrote the details down on paper and asked Dr. Paul to review our proposed strategy for starting IGMA.

The process of creating a nonprofit is housed in the Internal Revenue Service's Publication 557; however, the steps can be quite challenging. I was able to complete the task with little to no frustration because as a young adult I had obtained a grant writing certificate. Often people call me to help them start their nonprofit organization, and I have assisted several people over my adult lifetime.

Unfortunately, setting up nonprofits is not something I do on a regular basis and therefore, I have learned to call on the experts who have started thousands of successful nonprofit organizations.

To guide you in your own process, in Appendix 1, there is a direct link to the place that I used. That link takes you to Dr. William Paul's nonprofit organization website, called Church On The Road website. There, you'll find the complete details on how to start a nonprofit, if you feel impressed to start a nonprofit organization in memory of your loved one.

The steps are simple, but there are five main steps when starting a nonprofit. To generalize, in brief they are:

- Step 1: What will your nonprofit be?
- Step 2: Building a foundation for your organization
- Step 3: Becoming incorporated and filling out necessary state forms
- Step 4: Filing for federal tax-exempt status
- Step 5: Following ongoing compliance of the nonprofit

Every year, we remind our supporters regularly that our nonprofit organization has partnered with Alabama State University (ASU) to establish an endowment scholarship for ASU single parent learners (see Appendix 2). This annual fund is used to present educational scholarships in the amount of $1,000 during the Fall and Spring Semesters to deserving single parent students currently attending ASU and enrolled full time.

In the back of this book, there is a link with more information about our nonprofit, as well as where to find out more about the scholarships we award.

"When your name is called, what will be remembered about your story?"

"The way I used to view death was all wrong, instead I use my grief to find purpose bigger than my pain."

CHAPTER 3: IGMA INC

TURNING IN

What have I done to help keep the legacy alive?

What did I take from this chapter as I turn in and reflect?

What have I done, or can I start doing today to establish a nonprofit organization in memory of my loved one?

Chapter 3: IGMA Inc

Chapter 4: Faith

My faith, as I have come to understand it over the years of studying the Bible, is a process in my mind, in which I demonstrate my ability to believe things that I long to see manifested. Even when my eyes cannot see or touch my faith, I can see it in my everyday walk through life.

For example, my faith is what keeps me sane in the face of adversity. It has been built on countless hours of reading and studying God's unchanging word housed in the Holy Bible. While I am challenged in understanding the meaning behind every scripture, I have begun locating and using Bibles that make sense to me. For instance, the King James Version was quite difficult for me to grasp the many teachings because of the language used in the scriptures. So, I purchased a Good News Bible and a Message Bible to help me better understand the parables laid out in each of the sixty-six books of the Bible. While I realize each book has its significance, I constantly find myself returning to the lessons I have learned in my favorite books: Job, Proverbs, and Psalms.

Early after the death of my son, a host of my family and friends checked on me to see how I was doing. Many times I would respond with, "I am good", when in fact I was lying to both them and myself. Realizing that, I started a ritual of re-reading my favorite books of the Bible, hoping to achieve comfort. Most of the time I read and could not remember what I had read; I was simply calling out words. It wasn't until I began to study the word that I actually began to experience relief.

In other words, I made it a point to connect with others who were studying the Bible, as opposed to simply reading and calling out words. I visited in Sunday School and Bible study classes on a more regular basis. I committed to reading my Bible and reflecting on what I read daily. Over time, I allowed my faith in what I was reading to take shape and help me to reconnect in my belief in the word of God. I called on others who seemed to know the word much better than me.

At the same time, I had to caution myself from calling on those who would simply tell me what I wanted to hear. Although most meant well, I had to use my faith to shield me from those who felt sorry for me and welcomed my pity parties. So, I begin with greater intention my faith walk, gaining greater understanding of the Book of Job, the book of Proverbs, and the Book of Psalms.

Job

The Book of Job has exposed me to the importance of developing discernment. Through these verses, I learned the benefits of accepting those things in life for which I cannot control, such as my son's death. The Book of Job became an easy to read and understand guide about human suffering, though having a guide did not make the pain and suffering of losing my son any easier to stomach during the first few years.

The story of Job served as my example of one learning to endure in the midst of his trials and tribulations, although I found myself questioning God for answers to the age-old question of "Why". I felt many times that I had made God angry along life's journey and this was His way of punishing me, when in fact the Book of Job helped me to see I was not alone in questioning God.

In my study, I learned God looks beyond Job's fault of questioning Him; therefore, God would do the same for me. I was not there when the woman shot my son, but God was there with him and I do not have the whole picture. So, I found myself searching the Book of Job more and more to learn how Job established a level of hope. It took years before I could even begin to appreciate the endurance of Job, and God's promise to wipe away every tear from my eyes. I was also reminded in the Book of Job that death, mourning, crying, and pain would soon be no more. Although I cannot physically see my son today, I maintain my hope through continually reading and believing that I will see him again.

PROVERBS

The book of Proverbs has taught me to crave wisdom. Thus, I have come to value the lessons I have learned about how to behave in my daily walk of life. Each parable in the book of Proverbs seems to present me with instructions on how to gain wisdom, complete with practical applications for applying the wisdom I took from reading Proverbs. Heck, there were times when I fell down on my knees filled with so much pain that I actually cursed (cussed), screamed, and yelled at anyone who did not seem to understand my pain levels of grief.

Many times family and friends alike said things that hurt me to the core such as, "You need to try to stop thinking about him (Will) and try to pull yourself together. You need to stop going to visit the cemetery where your son is buried so often because it will help you get over the loss". Another said, "You know your son isn't at the cemetery, so what is the point in going so often?".

Trust and believe, I had no Sunday School words for people who did not get me. Although my response was initially "The hell with you. Who are you to tell me how I should feel?", in many instances, I would no longer call or take calls from people who felt they could try to tell me how I needed to grieve or not grieve. To decrease the pain felt often for days on end, I learned to use my daily reading of Proverbs to help me become a more effective communicator.

For example, each day, I read the Proverb that aligned with the day of the month and started the process over each month for years. I learned to apply the principle that I got from reading a Proverb lesson each day to the point where I understood what was meant when I read "I am teaching you today—yes you (me)—so you (me) will trust in the Lord" according to Proverbs 22:19 (New Living Translation).

The first six verses communicate the purpose of the book of Proverbs, and this was followed by me gaining a

CHAPTER 4: FAITH

greater understanding of my need to respect and take in the knowledge of God's Word. This study helped me fully understand how to apply the scriptures to my life.

When we become saved, we become filled with God's Holy Spirit. When studying the Bible, we become filled with God's Word, which is very much alive. Turning in is the act of turning toward God as He lives and breathes inside of us. There is comfort and peace in the scriptures, as well as guidance, especially in difficult times.

Therefore, turning in [to God] is the only way out [of grief / bondage]. Turning in to myself, I had to spend quality time with God daily to equip myself with the wisdom only He can give, and which I need each day to overcome those deep feelings of sorrow from having lost my beloved son. Through reading the book of Proverbs, I have been able to **G.R.O.W.** I have learned the value of: **G**oal setting, both long and short-term to achieve what I desire in life. **R**ecognizing my realities are not always as I have planned. **O**pening my heart to options, be it obstacles and/or opportunities in life. Lastly, that: **W**inning is my choice—and what is winning to me may be failure to others.

PSALMS

The Book of Psalms has taught me to lean not to my own understanding, but to turn to God for clarity in knowing who I am and what my purpose is for having been placed here on Earth. Most importantly, learned through reading Proverbs is how to be happy despite life's disappointments.

Chapter 4: Faith

Growing up as an adult, I began to learn who I am and my purpose.

The death of my son knocked me down for the count. I needed to rediscover who I was and my purpose for living and taking up space here on Earth. There were times I felt suicidal and had a strong desire to throw in the towel. It was not until the day I sat on the floor holding my daughter, whom I had almost shut out of my life because of the pain I was experiencing, that I realized I needed to learn how to be happy again. We cried profusely while holding each other and swaying side to side.

Star said, "Mom, you do so much for Bill (the name she and close relatives used for William), always working tirelessly doing things he will never see or know about. In case you have not noticed, I am right here. Sadly, we hardly talk, and you are not the only one who lost somebody—I lost my best friend."

With tears rolling down my face, I decided to do my best to not make her feel the terrible way I had grown accustomed to making her feel. So, I excused myself and fled to my bathroom. Once in there, I turned on the shower and screamed under the sounds of the shower water beating down on my face. While I stood limp in the shower, I realized not only did I need to read the Book of Psalms, but I had to hear the words.

I set up my phone to play the audio of Psalms while I continued to let the water run until it grew cold. During this hour, I believe I learned how to worship with God. After I dried off and put on my pajamas, I continued my praise and worship experience. I knelt down on my knees and then curled into a fetal position, asking God to help me overcome my feeling of pain and disappointment resulting from losing my son. I told God my heart was heavier than I could bear at that point in time.

Wholeheartedly, I believe God felt my pain and began to deal with me and my heartache in a manner that I had not experienced before. I realized in the days to come the importance of keeping a journal of my high and low experiences. This act helped me to view the Psalms as a blueprint for recording all my fears, levels of stress, pains, discomforts, and frustrations. These emotions had surfaced as a result of losing my son and feeling like a failure by making my daughter feel as if I did not love and appreciate her. Although I absolutely did not intentionally cause my feelings, they were all real to me.

Reading Psalms felt like déjà vu at times. It was as though someone had already known I would be at this place in my life. Now that I have frequently kept a journal of experiences during what felt like driving along a dark, endless highway, I feel empowered to share my story with those who may have or currently feel alone in a room full of people after having lost someone dear.

This empowerment required me to **E.V.O.L.V.E.** and I learned the importance of: **E**xercising my mind and body. **V**isualizing the end goal. **O**bserving by listening. **L**earning by applying knowledge. **V**olunteering when possible. **E**ndurance to the end. This became my mantra, and I firmly believed *quitting was not an option*.

CHAPTER 4: FAITH

This studying of the scriptures did not come without an additional set of challenges. As an educator for more than a dozen years, I must admit reading has not been my favorite pastime. With so many papers to read and grade and things to prepare for assignments, reading became less of an enjoyment and more of a chore. When I resumed reading after my son's death, it was more a way to temporarily block out any pain, than to actually absorb what I was reading. That's where I needed to make that change. How could I truly understand what the scriptures were teaching if I wasn't paying attention to what I was reading?

I have come to appreciate the Psalms because they present the scriptures like books of poetry. I have often wished the Book of Psalms could have been presented on an album. Whenever I ran across songs about the Psalms that made me want to dance, it was like music to my ears. In the back of the book, you'll find a list of my favorite songs, and the artists who created them, that were based on the Psalms and healing to me.

There have been so many songs that have provided me with strength and comfort, especially during the nights when my pillows have felt like a pool of cool water derived from my tears of sorrow. Each of these was instrumental in helping me as I moved forward. I knew the importance of needing to E.V.O.L.V.E. because there were too many times that I was slipping backward. So many days during this journey, I had to fight back the tears of hurt and disappointment of having to face another day without my son. I recall days of rolling out of bed and landing on my knees until I was able to plant my feet on the floor. At times,

CHAPTER 4: FAITH

I even stood, stretching out my hands up toward the sky and believing somehow, someway, my life was still in God's hand.

Occasionally I would fall asleep, discovering I had only closed my eyes for brief periods of time. My swollen eyes caused me to hide out in my room and go for days without eating because my sorrow was overwhelming. Each day, I would begin the cycle of praying and crying, crying and praying, until I was simply exhausted from sorrow and grief. My heart hurt and seemed to grow tired from the constant pain of losing my son. This pattern and thoughts of confinement lasted for weeks, months, and sometimes years, until someone would call to check on me, especially after I went through my divorce. Yes, in addition to grieving the death of William, there was yet another loss. I went through a divorce.

I was not capable then of mourning the loss of William and fighting for my marriage. My husband had tried to be supportive through my grief, but I'm not sure he knew how. Not long before, he had experienced the loss of his youngest daughter, and I wonder if it was just all too much.

On September 12, 2012, I received my divorce in the Cobb County courtroom. On the one hand, I was happy and sad on the other. I no longer had my son or my marriage. I was determined to overcome yet another loss. The struggle was challenging. I felt I was a failure and tried to hide the overwhelming feelings of hurt, even stopping to get a drink after leaving the courthouse to try and erase the shame I was feeling. It was to no avail. Instead, I went home and tried to sleep off the disappointment of feeling like a complete failure, as this was my second divorce.

I knew that the future would be brighter, that something better was ahead for me. I also knew that it would require me to become a better version of myself. The time was here. I must **B.E.C.O.M.E.** I realized what I needed to do, and the steps I had to take. I had to: **B**alance my time. **E**ncourage myself. **C**ommunicate effectively. **O**perate in excellence. **M**aster one goal at a time. **E**ducate and invest in myself!

As I implemented the E.V.O.L.V.E. and B.E.C.O.M.E. practices, I realized the importance of establishing a strong faith. I needed to see the next version of myself before it actualized. The only being who could make that possible was God.

My faith in God has been a major ingredient in helping me realize *Turning In Is the Only Way Out*. My faith has increased my commitment to praying, and not asking but thanking God for that which I need to strengthen me as I move forward. I thank Him in advance. He answers. There is great power in prayer.

My faith has led to a host of great affirmations which I wholeheartedly maintain have helped me to sustain my belief in God, despite life's disappointments. During my journey, I chose to write my affirmations on Post-It notes and strategically place them in places so that I would remember to read and repeat them daily. Because there were seven affirmations, I repeated at least one per day. The seven places where I placed my affirmations were on my bathroom mirror, my bedroom mirror, my refrigerator, on my computer monitor, on a cabinet near my kitchen sink, my other bathroom mirror, and on my car dashboard. Those were the places I most frequently visited each day. With one always nearby, I was reminded to read and speak at least one affirmation each day, which gave me a sense of peace, especially when I felt alone.

If you are struggling with grief, I strongly suggest you consider a similar meditational method. Writing, speaking, and reciting these affirmations will help when you are feeling low or downtrodden. You can create your own. If you need suggestions to get started, mine included:

- I have what I say I have, and I speak life into my situation.
- I love Jesus and Jesus loves me.
- I am an overcomer, and I can do all things because God strengthens me.
- I live my life seeking to serve others daily.
- I am a giver and not a taker.
- I am successful and everyone connected to me is a success.
- I am more than a conqueror, and no weapon formed against me shall prosper.
- My faith in God has positioned me to look into a fifth element of my belief, which is forgiveness.

"How do I measure my faith?"

TURNING IN

Where am I in my thoughts today about my faith after my loss?

What did I take from this chapter as I turn in and reflect?

What have I done, or can I start doing today to begin my faith strengthening journey?

CHAPTER 5: FORGIVENESS

When someone hurts me, intentionally or unintentionally, a natural response is to hurt them back. The sad part about forgiveness is that many people think a true measure of forgiveness is to forgive others. While forgiving others is important, I have learned that real forgiveness begins with forgiving oneself. Jeremiah 10:24 says, "O LORD, correct me, but with judgment; not in thine anger, lest thou bring me to nothing."

Although there is no timeline for when one person has to forgive another, I do know the sooner someone forgives, the sooner the healing process can begin. Forgiving someone is really not for the person who offended you. Instead, I learned forgiveness is for the person who has been offended. We are reminded in Ephesians 4:32, "And be ye kind one to another, tenderhearted, forgiving one another, even as God for Christ's sake hath forgiven you."

After [Perpetrator: KAJ] murdered my son, I felt as if I was carrying a heavy weight around my neck at the mere mention of her name. I wanted to seek immediate revenge because the hatred and hurt in my heart seemed unbearable. My shoulders would tense up as if I was dragging a ton of bricks, until the day sitting at a 45-degree angle behind her at the first hearing of the murder trial.

After the announcement that this would be moved to a grand jury, at first I still sat in the courtroom because I did not know what I needed to do next. The judge repeated what he had said, and I finally got the strength in my legs to leave the courtroom. Also, I sat there so long because I heard the voice of the Lord clearly say to me, "Now you need to go and FORGIVE her."

When I heard those words, I did not move. I said nothing. I began to internalize because I could not believe the Lord was instructing me to FORGIVE this woman for having murdered my son. A scripture came to mind, Matthew 6:14, "For if ye forgive men their trespasses, your heavenly Father will also forgive you." Talk about Lord help my unbelief! Trust and believe, I thought to myself, God has the wrong person. Besides, she and her attorney had already left the courtroom. I felt the request from God was not possible. Yet to ensure God's Word was clear, I said, "Okay, God. But if she is gone when I get outside, then I won't have to forgive her."

Gathering myself, I headed out to the lobby, followed by Star and Keta. To make good on my promise, I walked right up to my son's shooter with tears in my eyes and said, "I forgive you". There was a still moment. She was as shocked to hear me say I forgive you, as I was to have said it to her.

Meanwhile, my Star and Keta were behind me like bodyguards, each appearing to take off their earrings because they thought we were about to get into an altercation. The two imagined the old Angelia was back. The one who would go to bat for her family to kick butt and take names as a last resort. It was at that moment that I realized the true meaning of FORGIVENESS.

Psalms 145:8 says, "The LORD *is* gracious, and full of compassion; slow to anger, and of great mercy." This was a time that I needed to be each of those things. It was hard. Absolutely. Standing there looking at this woman was one of the most difficult things I have ever done. Keeping my composure was about all I could do at that point. Yet, I had made a conscious decision to take back my power of resentment and vengeance I had stored up, despite the fact this woman had taken the life of my son with what appeared to be no remorse. At that time, in my heart, I did not believe she deserved to be forgiven.

Over time, I realized forgiving the shooter was my first opportunity to gain a sliver of peace of mind and free myself from the initial place of bondage and confinement. In Psalms 30:5, we are taught "For his anger endureth but a moment; in his favour is life: weeping may endure for a night, but joy cometh in the morning." While I do not have any positive feelings for or toward the woman who killed my son, I did feel the bricks crumble from my shoulders. These stones that had me weighed down had kept me pinned and unable to heal and move on with my life. Without forgiveness, I was walking dead at the hands of this woman.

Honestly speaking, forgiving her was not an easy task. It was, however, made easier because my pastor had successfully been preaching a series on forgiveness at church. Under Pastor Purvis' leadership, I learned how important it is as a believer to equip myself with knowledge and understanding of the word. In other words, knowledge has no power until it is applied. I believe God knew I needed to understand the full breadth and depth of the word

CHAPTER 5: FORGIVENESS

FORGIVENESS, and the means by which I must demonstrate how to forgive others.

Today, my advice to someone needing to know how to forgive is simple. Forgiveness is important. It is for you, not just for those you are forgiving. I recommend first committing to accepting Christ in your heart. Believe without a shadow of a doubt that Christ died for your sins, and confess your sins to God so that He can forgive you. Together, this is the plan of salvation made simple. For I am reminded, according to Matthew 6:12, "and forgive us our sins, as we have forgiven those who sin against us."

Once you have accepted, believed, and confessed according to the Holy Bible, then your heart is ready to forgive others. Forgiving of the woman who killed my son entailed me researching and gaining knowledge and insight about the concept. I learned much, and felt enriched by the new teachings I obtained. Afterwards, I followed the seven-step process I uncovered in my research by Negroni (2013, December 10), published three years after my son's murder. It's titled, "7 Steps to True Forgiveness".[2]

These steps helped me to establish a sense of resolve. I applied these steps to every aspect of my daily life. To help you in your own journey, I'd like to share each of those steps, but also in what way it helped me. As you read each of these 7 steps, personalize them to your own specific situation. Ponder what will help you to heal in your

---

[2] Negroni, J. (2013, Dec 10) 7 Steps to True Forgiveness. Retrieved https://thriveworks.com/blog/7-steps-to-true-forgiveness/

suffering. Take the time to really think about what each of these steps means for you personally, why it's so important, and how it can help you as you move forward.

- ➢ **Acknowledge**: I suffered deeply as a parent at the hands of a stranger who murdered my son in the prime of his young life.

- ➢ **Consider**: I took time to think how I might never find peace if I allowed the negative impacts of the shooter's inconsiderate actions to hold me in a hostage state of mind.

- ➢ **Accept**: I could not change the outcome of having lost my son, nor did I have a way to punish the one who killed him to ease the pain.

- ➢ **Determine**: When thinking about the next step, forgiveness was clearly the direction I needed to take at that point in my life. Otherwise, it felt as if she had pulled the same trigger on me, however, I never died nor healed from my wound.

- ➢ **Repair**: My internal relationship needed to be repaired through my action of saying in person to the shooter, "I forgive you". Remember, forgiveness is not just for those who have wronged us, but for us as well.

- ➢ **Learn**: With tears in my eyes, I realized forgiving this woman benefited me. That burden of bricks I had been carrying no longer felt as heavy to me. It was in that moment, I realized I was on the path to restoration. By the same, I learned time would eventually lead me to closure.

➢ **Forgive:** The act of forgiving the woman who shot my son essentially marked the start of my silent healing journey. I did not expect her to respond when I gave her my forgiveness, although I believe to this day God used that moment in time to position me to move on from the captivity of my grief.

"Holding on to unforgiveness prevents me from achieving a place of resolution and peace."

CHAPTER 5: FORGIVENESS

TURNING IN

Where am I in my thoughts about my forgiveness today?

What did I take from this chapter as I turn in and reflect?

What have I done, or can I start doing today to begin my forgiveness strengthening journey?

Chapter 6: Family

My family are those who make up the group of people related to me by blood or by marriage and who have supported me since we met. C. B. Griffin Jr was a former councilman to some, but for me, my father was a hero who instilled in me the need to serve others and be true to myself no matter what the world thought of me. My awesome daddy taught me the importance of community and family. He was my rock and number one fan, and loved my son almost as if he gave him life. To know my dad and my son now share the same heavenly residence is refreshing, despite the fact that both my dad and my son have transitioned to be with the Lord.

I am also very thankful for the relationship I developed with my godfather, John Dublin Matthews (Coach), namely because he also played an intricate part in helping me to regain my footing resulting from the loss of my son. He reminded me of the importance of living a life free of a lot of stress. I will always remember and share with others his famous recipe he shared with me often for enjoying years of a happy life: Pay my bills, take my pills, and read daily Psalms 23, 37, 91, and 100.

In the back pages of this book, you'll find the names of others who supported me. Each is valuable, and each was so needed, however I want to take a moment to talk more about the importance of family in general.

After a tragedy, your family is often who you turn to first. These are the ones who know you and accept you and love you where you are, and how you are. They are the ones you can turn to in tears and sorrow, joy and memories. While relationships can vary between our family members, there are hopefully a few that you know you can rely on should you need them.

At times, when there's been a death, illness, or other life-changing event, you'll find that there are those who rush forward to help, but also those who hold back a little. This holding back doesn't mean that you aren't loved, that they don't want to help. It's more that they might not know how. They don't know what to say, how to act—it could even be that something difficult has just happened to them, but they aren't mentioning it because they don't want to make you feel as though your situation isn't important.

Although you might not be fully capable of comprehending the type of help you need and when, perhaps another family member does know, and could take charge, setting up things like meal trains, transportation for other family members, or for grocery deliveries. It could even be that you need help with the absolute basics of your day. Laundry, dishes, taking care of phone calls, or making arrangements for the situation you are in. Some of those things that just have to get done, but we aren't quite in the right frame of mind to do yet.

Being with family in a time of sorrow is a balm to the soul. They can uplift you in a way no other can. So closely you are connected, it's a chance to be yourself and share your heart and your tears, both of joy and sadness.

CHAPTER 6: FAMILY

Without a doubt, each of the people in my family has afforded me the opportunity to share my perfect and not so perfect days. In our conversations, I've talked about my son, sharing stories of what I missed most about him. Many of the conversations were refreshing and needed, helping me deal with the fact that Will's transition of life was not expected, yet family became my unwavering source of love and support.

I began to repeat the following love reminders, which helped me to recall the good qualities of my amazing son whom I miss and will always love. **W.I.L.L.P.: W**ork, **I**nspire, **L**ive, **L**ife, **P**lease! These letters are engraved on his headstone, and each letter stands for a way he was special to me: **W**orked to always be a breath of fresh air. **I**nspired me by always having my back. **L**ived to love and care. **L**ife was centered around his mom and son. **P**lease pray that I will one day get over the love we shared for one another.

Having these love reminders helps me to feel close to my son. If you have lost a loved one, it is certain that you also have reminders of what they loved to do, how they acted, how they cared for others or inspired. Is there a phrase you can create to help you remember them, or to inspire or encourage you when you are feeling at a low point?

Life has its moments of difficulty. Yet at this moment in time, I am grateful to share that I have exhaled and now I can breathe. My family, have each continued to undergird me in ways I never knew I needed from each of them.

Although I sometimes miss the mark, I do my best to thank them and remind them I appreciate their love and support during my darkest days here on Earth as a mother. Family is incredibly important. I hope that you have a family you can call on to support you. Sometimes just knowing there is someone you can talk to, cry with, and lean on can make all the difference in the world on a healing journey. If you are not blessed to have family nearby and able to help, in the next chapter I talk about friends, and how they can be a support system for you as well.

"Work, Inspire, Live Life, Please!"

CHAPTER 6: FAMILY

TURNING IN

Where am I in my thoughts about my family today?

What did I take from this chapter as I turn in and reflect on my family?

What have I done, or can I start doing today to begin my family strengthening journey?

Chapter 6: Family

Chapter 7: Friends

Friends are the non-related individuals who pass My **L.A.S.H.3C.3P Litmus Test,** which defines my true friends as those who are:

- **L**oyal
- **A**ccepting
- **S**upportive
- **H**onest
- **C**aring
- **C**ommitted
- **C**omforting
- **P**resent
- **P**ositive and
- **P**atient

… with me despite my flaws. However, as a friend once reminded, friends are like closets. Sometimes you simply have to clean them out in order to decipher between the good and the bad. I have come to realize that just because someone classifies you as his or her friend, not all definitions of a friend hold true.

At the same time, I am thankful there are different types of friends, each who has his or her own set of unique qualities. Not everyone is fortunate enough to have family nearby. Sometimes these friends become our family. And while not everyone is blessed to have close friends, or those who live near, it is my hope you have at least a few you know you can rely on. Friendship comes in levels, have you noticed? I see that is true for myself. There are the friends I speak to occasionally, but we are able to pick up our conversations right from where we last left off. Other times, a friend is one who you text or phone often, see frequently in a shared interest (like a class, church, or workplace). Perhaps your conversations are not as deep or as intimate, but they are still a companion, nonetheless.

When my son passed away, I experienced several types of varying support in my friendships. There were my longtime friends, many of whom I did not hear from. Some reached out to me with a casual checking in to see how I was, while others proved to be unfriendly in my healing journey.

Just as with family members offering different levels of support, the same can be said of friendships. While ideally, it would be wonderful if you could expect your friends to be an endless well of help, hope, and comfort, there are few who can fill those needs. Perhaps it's that they don't know how to offer that support you need. Maybe they are concerned they will say the wrong thing, and would rather pull back than risk upsetting you more. It could even be that they have their own serious concerns, yet don't want to mention them.

It is my hope that you are blessed with the kinds of friends I call "ride or die", namely because they have been with me and remained with me through the good times and the bad, especially those dark times when I first lost my son. Knowing the levels of friendships I had allowed me to become more comfortable around my friends, especially in what requests I could make or support I could ask for. I knew I could freely ask for certain things from particular individuals, and they wouldn't mind the request. At times, I didn't even have to ask, they simply knew me well enough to know what it was I needed, or were able to offer assistance in ways I didn't even realize how valuable it was, until it was offered.

Learning how each friend has a unique place in my world has made me more confident in knowing these friends are very important to my continued growth. A good friend has such value. They are not only a support system during difficult times, but they also serve as role models, inspiration, and create a way to deepen those relationships, as you each discover new things about the other, and come to help, bless, and evolve as a human being.

I am blessed to have acquired a host of acquaintances throughout my lifetime. While I do not recall every person by name, I owe a debt of gratitude to those who have remained with me to date. Collectively, my friends have been instrumental in helping me define my self-worth, which positioned me to keep my eyes on the prize while striving to empower others and myself. Sadly, I may have missed out on opportunities to add to my list of friends due to my depression, almost to a point where I was attempting to bury myself alive in self-pity. Thankfully, if you keep your heart open, and seek out new faces to talk to, those friendships come.

A few years before my son's death, my daughter and I moved our worship membership to an amazing, thriving church under the authentic leadership of Wilbur T. Purvis III, our Senior Pastor. Little did I know when I connected with the Destiny World Church family and its body of believers, I would walk out with the words that had prepared me for the time in which I had to bury my son. Although each sermon I experienced offered great opportunities to hear dynamic life-changing messages, one of my favorites was received through connecting with people from all walks of life, entitled "Forgiveness".

At the time of the message, I did not realize how influential the contents of the sermon would be on my life at the time of my son's death. The sermon encouraged me to be more intentional in all that I do, although the spiritual journey that brought me to this bus stop in my life did not come without a host of growing pains.

Honestly, I was not only hurt and scared when I first got the call regarding the fatal shooting of my son, I was also angry. The reason was not solely because I learned my son had been shot, but I also realized in the days to come, I did not have my affairs in order. Like many parents and guardians, I never imagined having to bury one of my children.

In early 2010, before William's death, I did try to establish a life insurance policy for each of my children. Sadly, I allowed life's challenges to let me procrastinate in my quest

CHAPTER 7: FRIENDS

to look for an appropriate insurance plan that fit my financial budget. This was in part because both William and Star were away at college and I did not have any disposable money. Nonetheless, I promised myself I would make it my priority to get them insured.

A few months later, in August 2010, I reached out to my life insurance agent of twenty-plus years to schedule a time when both my children would be down in Peachtree City at their father's home to complete the screening and paperwork for their policies. Once the paperwork was completed, I was told the next steps would be handled by a person whom I considered a professional friend, an insurance agent whom I prefer to keep nameless because we are no longer in communication. This individual proved to be less than a friend when I needed him the most.

A couple of days after my son passed away, I reached out only to learn the agent had not processed the final steps of the paperwork. The policy that I thought was in place was not completed, which meant I did not have a way to properly bury my son as I had planned.

Over the next six months, I undertook seeking a re-evaluation of my son's life insurance policy. Thankfully, in the end, a decision was made to overturn the initial denial and to pay the policy without delay. To God be the glory, because without the support of my Destiny World Church family, I would not have been able to afford to bury my son with a level of dignity and meet the financial obligations at the time of the funeral while I awaited the processing of the funds due.

CHAPTER 7: FRIENDS

I appreciate all the people whose paths I've crossed over the years. It is both a humbling and eye-opening experience to realize how much I needed each of them, and in different ways. In this space where I have learned to operate, I realized, these men and women proved to be my sheroes and heroes during my darkest hours as a recovering, hurting adult. There are not enough words in my vocabulary to communicate the role each played in getting me to where I stand in my life today. Thus, I can only hope and pray our heavenly father will render uncommon favor for all that they did to help me get back on my feet and realize my self-worth.

There is a benefit to establishing a core group of people who will make time to listen when life happens. Ones who will respect you enough to know when you say no, you may just need a little space to gather yourself. They'll never tell you what you want to hear, rather than what you need to hear, and be okay with being silent when there are no words to say to express your thoughts. It is also important to note that some friends might even be the ones we least expect to be there for us, but who are. Don't be quick to dismiss the help or support of any, especially if you are at a point in life where help will make things better for you. Give others the opportunity to serve and bless, as you will later do for another.

While not all of my friends share their personal relationships with me, in my heart, I wish for each blessing that renders a return for their many sacrifices to show me love at a time when I had forgotten how to love myself. I learned to live out my favorite quote by Eddie A. Rios, who once stated: *"I cheated on my fears, broke up with my doubts, got engaged to my faith, and now I am marrying my dreams! Soon I will be holding hands with my Destiny!"*

As I grow in my faith, I seek to be forgiven for times when I lost my way in life, especially in the eyes of my friends. How grateful I am for their uplifting support in my time of need. Because of them, I have the strength to continue on my path. My focus is on God's plan, purpose, promise, and provision, and I chose to make each day all about me.

*"My L.A.S.H.3C.3P Litmus Test
defines my true friends"*

CHAPTER 7: FRIENDS

TURNING IN

Where am I in my thoughts today about my true friends?

What did I take from this chapter as I turn in and reflect?

What have I done or can I start doing today to begin my friendships strengthening journey?

Chapter 8: Food (E.A.T.I.N.G.)

Who would have thought food could be the difference in helping me to heal? At first, I certainly did not see this essential as a way to find my way back to feeling whole again. Yet, food is a nourishing substance taken into the body to sustain life, provide energy, and promote growth. Just like the support from family and friends, food would become an essential part of my healing journey.

When reflecting on my food consumption, I realized my eating habit was in a class all by itself. My nutritional needs have included four main categories. I have always enjoyed eating religiously: Breakfast, lunch, dinner, and snacks. Over the years, each has provided me with solid nourishment, which in turn helped me to enjoy life daily. My friends, family and acquaintances know me as the person who enjoys eating four to five times a day.

Prior to my son's death, I loved to start my day around 7:00 am, eating a well-balanced breakfast which consisted of a nice size bowl of cheese grits, two cheese-scrambled eggs, two slices of raisin toast, in-season fruit, and a small glass of cranberry or apple juice. At about 10:00 am, I enjoyed a light snack which usually included an apple, grapes, or an orange. Between the hours of 1 and 2 pm, I usually liked to sit down to a peanut butter and jelly sandwich and a nice size glass of cold milk, which often helped me to make it to my dinner time which I ate between 7 and 8 pm, and often included vegetables, a meat, a couple of rolls, rice, and gravy. Often, I ate my dessert between 9 and 10 pm, even on the weekends.

Some of my peers, family, friends, and acquaintances thought my consumption of food appeared excessive, and I have been referred to as "greedy." The blessing of eating four or five times a day is housed in the fact that I have always had a very high metabolism, which supported my ability to consume a lot of food. My weekend food regimen almost mirrored my weekday habits, except for indulging in waffles, homemade biscuits, and buttermilk pancakes.

Someone reading this book might be wondering why I classified food as one of my eight essentials. Well, the answer can be summed up in three points. First, I love food and eating four to five times a day seemed quite normal until I lost my son. Second, I realize food provides a great comfort to me when I am stressed, especially when I am all alone. Third, food for me never was a thought. Because my metabolism has always been very high, I could get away with eating whatever and whenever I wanted.

That all changed. The day I lost William, I also lost any interest in eating. The loss of appetite and lack of desire for any nourishment grew to the point people who knew me began to worry that I had truly lost my way and the will to keep living. I would eat maybe once, but no more than twice a day and nothing more than a couple bites of a sandwich or maybe a small piece of fruit between the tears. To say the least, I began to develop a very unhealthy schedule of eating habits. I craved a piece of chocolate candy and something sweet to drink when I did find the desire to put

Chapter 8: Food (E.A.T.I.N.G)

a little something in my mouth during the weeks and months of grieving the loss of William.

At the time, it felt like my world had come to a screeching halt and there really was no reason to care about myself, let alone eating habits. I wanted to die physically, because I felt like I had already died inside and the neglect of my body and mind were easier to do than to feed myself. Eating was no longer fun, nor something I enjoyed doing. In like manner, I no longer enjoyed exercising. Everything was too much effort, and I just didn't see the point of going to the trouble.

I simply did not care about anything else as I grieved the loss of my son. William's death left me empty and unwilling to even want to do the things in life that used to be basic. Before long, I found sleeping and crying to be the best way to cope.

The day came when I had to go in for my annual physical and my physician asked me how I was doing. Tears rolling down my face, I opened up, saying to her, "My heart hurts. I feel tired and I have no energy at all. I am often exhausted, restless, impatient, sometimes my stomach aches, my head hurts, I have trouble sleeping, and I realize I am more irritable than in the past."

We talked for a while. After taking all my vitals, she recommended a change in my hypertension medication and the inclusion of vitamin D once a week. My weight had decreased tremendously, and I felt dizzy and tired. We spoke a little longer and discussed my eating habits, which were different from what others were accustomed to, knowing me as the human food garbage disposal.

My physician explained that high metabolism is something many people wished they had, and regardless of having one or not, it was important to still get enough calories a day. She recalled a number of conversations about enjoying foods, like my favorites: liver, rice, and gravy, with onions and garden peas, all of which had their rightful place according to my body's ability to break such foods down with ease. Unfortunately, by not eating, I was causing health problems for myself. Not only was I experiencing weight loss, increased hypertension, migraine headaches, sleepless nights, and stress, but all of this could be prevented by one thing. Food.

We don't realize it, but enough nourishment in our bodies really plays an enormous role in our overall health. I was told I needed to eat healthier to avoid low blood sugar levels and feelings of highs and lows, which were my body's way of screaming I needed food. The mere morsels I was putting in my body were simply not enough and not helping me positively go through my grieving process.

Shortly after my physical was when I had my divorce, and with it went my health coverage. For a few years, I took the physician's advice and played health provider for myself until I simply could not fight any more. I searched for a discount medical coverage which I could afford. Although it was not a top-of-the-line coverage, it did afford me the opportunity to return to my great doctor's care. I got back on top of the importance of taking the right blood pressure medication on a consistent basis, and establishing proper eating habits.

Talking to others and increasing my knowledge while attending "Google University" (the World Wide Web) I took it upon myself to better understand the importance of eating right. I also learned eating unhealthily is not uncommon among those who are deeply saddened by the unexpected loss of a loved one. It can be a coping mechanism, one which can become a habit. However, when I began to eat healthier, the sadness and pain I was feeling slowly diminished. Eating healthy, nourishing meals on a more consistent basis served to be an essential testament to my *Turning In* journey during the grieving process.

Today, healthy eating consists mostly of oatmeal or cereal for breakfast. A sandwich, fruit, and pretzels for lunch along with a well-balanced dinner and medium size portions that are not high in calorie counts. I love my fruits and vegetables because I have noticed they help me to control my mood swings.

Eating home prepared meals has helped diminish my days of sadness because I focus during meal preparation on the good times I experienced while preparing my son's favorite meals. I try to minimize my fast food intake, having come to learn the importance of eating less processed food and more fresh produce and seasonal vegetables, especially the leafy green ones, and all types of nuts. I eat very few canned foods and no microwavable dinners. I have never indulged in a cup of coffee, although I will drink a cup of cocoa or cappuccino.

Chapter 8: Food (E.A.T.I.N.G)

When it comes to sweets, those are also now in moderation. Bread is my vice; however, potato bread seems to be healthier over that of white and wheat breads for me. My beverage intake typically includes four to six eight-ounce bottles of water each day and an occasional ginger ale or Sprite during the week. I learned early in my grieving that alcohol and I do not mix well. It either causes me to fall into a deep sleep or else everything becomes very funny, and I am the only one laughing in the room.

The decision I made to eat healthier has been one of the greatest decisions ever made. While I do not care about what people say or think about me as I travel along my grief journey, I am concerned about how I feel and value my self-worth. Eating is still my vice. There is still a struggle at times. However, I simply research and read labels to help me better understand and choose better options. I check in with my physician regularly to ensure I am being held accountable to the prescribed regimen for healthier living for my body. The more I learn, I realize there is value in taking walks, meditating, getting proper sleep, and eating a consistent and well-balanced meal a couple of times throughout each day.

Another benefit to healthy eating and preparing meals at home is it lessens stress levels. We can all get so busy and overwhelmed, especially in the evenings. Something I do that really helps with that evening meal stress is to take the time to prepare several days' worth of meals, freeze them in portions, and warm them up in foil as opposed to throwing them in the microwave when I am ready to eat. I find value in planning my weekly meals, which lessens the need to stress myself with making daily decisions.

Most importantly, I have discovered eating healthy has helped to decrease my levels of grief, while positioning me to regain the desire to engage with others and face the unknowns of the grieving process. I truly believe there is no set time for when or how to overcome a feeling of loss, but I do know I have the strength to keep fighting the good fight, which helps me to overcome any self-pity or victim mentality that might occur.

So far, tying these healthy eating habits to the many good times I experience with others helps me create new memories and helps me cope with the loss of my amazing son. In fact, we have even made new traditions for us all to gather and celebrate together, assigning a new memory to foods or places associated with my son. It's one no less filled with joy, but instead of pain and sadness when recalling a food or place, there is happiness. For example, every year, my family and I celebrate Will's life on his birthday by eating something he loved or at one of his favorite restaurants. This turns the day into one of happiness, fellowshipping, and remembrance, not a day of sorrow and loss.

Throughout this chapter, you may have noticed that food and eating are terms I use synonymously. Eating is more than a time to nourish the body. Foods vary, but eating has turned into a comforting acronym: **E.A.T.I.N.G.** This helped remind me of what I needed to do, the things I already knew, and that there was a way to move forward. While I learned this the long way, the hard way, I wish for you not to suffer as I have while learning to cope with the loss of a loved one. Change these as you need to, so that it can fit your particular situation or person.

Express moments of sadness and share thoughts with close family and friends. Often they are received as conversation without judgment.

Accept the fact that my son is not coming back, although I long to receive just one text or phone call from him.

Treat myself to a meal in his honor or think about something he did to make me smile or laugh since we often connected over a meal or talking on the phone.

Invite others to participate in initiatives with our nonprofit to remember and share the passion Will had for helping others, especially youth and seniors.

Never forget to celebrate Will's birthday or homegoing day. Fresh flowers are put on his grave every year on his birthday. Annually, funds are raised to give out educational scholarships.

Give of myself to empower others through our 501c3 established in memory of my son, who gave his life to prevent someone else from losing theirs.

I encourage anyone who has experienced the loss of a loved one, expected or unexpected, to consider implementing my E.A.T.I.N.G. strategies as a way to overcome the hurt you may be feeling or have felt while

CHAPTER 8: FOOD (E.A.T.I.N.G)

coping. These strategies have provided me with a path to happiness that I never imagined.

If I can be of assistance to you as you are E.A.T.I.N.G. your way back to a life filled with joy, please contact me to talk about how to get started as you journal the way you want to remember the good times you had with your loved one.

"The way I view food has taught me the importance of E.A.T.I.N.G. healthy."

CHAPTER 8: FOOD (E.A.T.I.N.G)

TURNING IN

Where am I in my thoughts today about my E.A.T.I.N.G?

What did I take from this chapter as I turn in and reflect?

What have I done, or can I start doing today to begin my food strengthening journey?

CHAPTER 9: FIDUCIARY RESPONSIBILITY

In my quest to overcome bondage and confinement resulting from the most painstaking loss imaginable, I turned in to figure out how to live again. Although I never asked God why my son had to leave the Earth, I did often ask, "How do I pick up the pieces and move on in life?" Night after night I would drop off to sleep and wake to a fully tear drenched pillow, struggling with the whole idea of grief from loss, and the uncertainty of how to live with it.

Early in my journey, I thought about throwing in the towel of life because the pain was simply unbearable. I wondered when I would smile again. Was there happiness still in life? What was a step I could take to move forward? How could I honor my son?

As the years after Will's death passed, I often gazed at others interacting with their children. Observing them, I'd think to myself, the reason my son's life was taken was because of my poor choices as a parent, starting with my choice to divorce his father. I experienced a lot of guilt. Eventually, I realized I could not stay in the confined state of mind I had found myself. I needed to identify a path forward.

After several years of blaming myself for William's death and searching for peace after countless days and nights on my knees, the day came to be released from my bondage and confinement. Writing this book was like watering parched, brown grass. I felt if I simply sat down at my

CHAPTER 9: FIDUCIARY RESPONSIBILITY

computer and began with a simple prayer, "God show me how to live again" the Lord's will would prevail. I had faith in that. And it did.

The feeling came that it was time to stop trying to give purpose to my son's being. Truthfully, I had been holding myself hostage until I thought I could present my son's purpose to the world. It was my main focus, my goal, and it was something I tried to do above all else, and each day. I have experienced more than what I feel is one person's share of grief in my quest to try and live through my son. For the past ten years, I have done my best to bring about an awareness of him, hoping to invoke a change in society regarding bullying and gun violence.

Others have also worked to keep momentum going for awareness of this serious topic. I invited my daughter to take an active role in our nonprofit organization and she graciously accepted the call. Our IGMA executive board members agreed to establish our annual Certified Good Deeds Educational Scholarship as a special tribute in memory of William Donald Paul II, for his commitment in encouraging and inspiring other youth and young adults to appreciate individual self-worth.

As I explained briefly in Chapter 1, each year, six students receive a scholarship, but to further help Will's legacy and to build their own and give back to the community, there is a stipulation. Recipients must agree to participate as a volunteer through IGMA initiatives or some other 501c3 nonprofit organization(s) dedicated to social change or related challenges facing our ever-changing society.

Chapter 9: Fiduciary Responsibility

As the founder and president of I Give Myself Away, Inc, I am pleased to share that through our nonprofit, and partnerships with individuals and organizations who are also striving to empower others, I have found purpose bigger than my pain. IGMA has afforded the opportunity to channel hurts into opportunities, allowing me to encourage others.

A believer in Jesus Christ, I have also been afforded the opportunity to share my story and positively influence others who may have or are presently walking in my shoes. I am convinced that my loss of William has allowed me to help others who have unexpectedly and/or tragically lost a child, especially due to senseless gun violence. Having walked this path before other grieving parents puts me in a position to reach out with compassion, understanding, and love.

To come to this point, though, I first had to see myself as an overcomer with a heart and realize it is okay to *not* be okay, for however long I needed to take in order to feel whole again. There is no time limit on grief. Each of us grieves and heals differently, and in a different time frame. As I knew my son would never come back, and nothing I did could change that, I became relentlessly committed to my strong desire to empower others. It was time to focus my energies on making a difference and empowering other young men and women to have better circumstances.

I am privileged to work with a group of women IGMA officers who support me in my decision to stand tall as we work to help those who need our support and efforts. Over the years, I have learned that part of my responsibility isn't just to others, it's to myself. It has been a conscious decision each morning to wake up and know that I must choose how my day will be and how I will react. I decided that I am no longer a victim because I am more than a conqueror according to the scriptures. Every day, it is my responsibility to get up with an attitude of gratitude and seek ways to empower others instead of dwelling on the negatives in my life.

In this era of social media and instant gratification, it's easy for anyone to get swept up into a mindset of feeling like something is due, and due in a particular time frame. After all, Amazon promises us two-day shipping, so why did it take three days when we were promised two? A pizza delivery—shouldn't it be less than thirty minutes? These thoughts start small, but can grow. I realized the world does not owe me anything. Instead, it is my job to leave a positive impression on each individual I interact with.

Forgiving the person who wronged me was necessary, as was forgiving myself for feeling helpless and unable to protect my son from the ignorant behaviors of others. Forgiveness is a crucial key to healing. It's a needed gift for yourself, as much, if not more, than it is for others. We are each responsible for our own happiness. Eventually, I realized that blaming others for my shortcomings needed to stop. This personal acceptance and responsibility are a part of maturity. Life's lessons will help build character if they do not kill me, I always say!

Chapter 9: Fiduciary Responsibility

Part of my responsibility to empower and help others has come through my ability to leverage personal and professional experiences on a weekly radio show called *All That Matters*. This method is used to discuss and educate listeners on topics pertaining to business, legal matters, education, nonprofits, technology, and healthcare. Radio has become my new platform, one which affords me an amazing opportunity to interview guest speakers (ordinary people doing extraordinary things) and carry out the IGMA mission of empowering others despite my personal loss.

Running an effective nonprofit organization is a process that requires constant collaboration with our board of directors and a commitment to the realignment of my efforts and thoughts with the organization's stated mission and vision. It's difficult, challenging, and on occasion, time consuming or stressful, but I refuse to think about the negative aspects. There are no negative aspects because the goal of IGMA is to help others, and that brings me much joy and fulfillment.

Establishing supporters for any organization, requires the ability to be steadfast and immovable toward the goal of building relationships. This means that there are times I must remember the importance of putting an *L* in front of my *ego* to become a *Lego*. Think about a Lego. On its own, one of those small plastic bricks can't do much. You need several pieces combined to build something amazing. It's the same with creating a relationship. In order to be successful, I must constantly and consistently build and grow each day for the rest of my life.

Chapter 9: Fiduciary Responsibility

This also means I must endeavor to avoid intentionally hurting others. As I have learned, hurt people are known for hurting others. They are quicker to lash out defensively to prevent more hurt, when they are not trying to hurt others to make themselves feel better. It doesn't matter if it's a stranger, family member, or friend. We can each act that way on occasion. In fact, not all who profess to be a true friend are. I'm sure you've experienced that at some point in your life. Some have ulterior motives and will occasionally seek to manipulate. Like many, I have not always operated in a place of sound judgment in my life. It's easy during a time of heightened emotion to make a choice that isn't actually the best one to have made.

While moving forward, I desired to be the change I wished to see in other moms who may have experienced, or were experiencing, the type of hurt I knew. I made a conscious decision to share my journey and communicate my 8 Essential Ingredients of peace, joy, happiness, and wholeness, which are outlined in this book and explained in each chapter. Delving deep into these has helped me to overcome a deep feeling of confinement.

I have regained the ability to smile despite having suddenly and tragically lost my only son. This brokenhearted mother has been on a journey out of bondage and into a place of wholeness.

These 8 Essential Ingredients are:

- Faith
- Forgiveness

Chapter 9: Fiduciary Responsibility

- Family
- Friends
- Food
- Fiduciary Responsibility
- Finance
- Fear

Muhammad Ali said, "Service to others is the rent we pay for the space we occupy here on Earth". It's absolutely true. As you move forward on your own journey out of bondage, take time to consider, prayer, and discuss with others how these essential elements—Faith, Forgiveness, Family, Friends, Food, Fiduciary Responsibility, Finance, and Fear—can bring you into a better place and a new journey. One where you are whole, healed, and recognize you have the strength and ability to help others and teach them that there is life and happiness to be had after a loss.

Remember, it is okay not to be okay, as healing is an individual journey!

CHAPTER 9: FIDUCIARY RESPONSIBILITY

TURNING IN

Where am I in my thoughts today about my fiduciary responsibilities?

What did I take from this chapter as I turn in and reflect?

What have I done, or can I start doing today to begin my fiduciary strengthening journey?

Chapter 10: Finances

I was taught to save money and prepare for a rainy day. However, like many, financial words of wisdom did not hold my undivided attention in my early years. Now, when I reflect on my younger years, I realize I did not always value the wisdom shared by my parents.

Sad but true, I am guilty of having spent more than I brought home because I did not want to let the money I had burn a hole in my pocket. In fact, I never placed great value in preparing for a rainy day until faced with how to bury my son. To further complicate the financial situation, I assumed that if I simply completed the final expense paperwork for my children, that would be enough. There was no need to further save, prepare, or plan. After all, I did not plan to bury my child, just as no parent plans to bury a child.

For the most part, my finances had been predicated on living from one paycheck to the next. For a long time, I was embarrassed to admit I did not have my financial affairs in order. If back then I managed my finances with what I now know today, I would have made sure I prepared for the unfortunate tragic death of my son by establishing insurance coverage with a policy when my children were younger. Although there is no amount of money that can suffice for my loss, knowing I could have put my son to rest with dignity and no stress might have offered me a piece of peace.

CHAPTER 10: FINANCES

I also would have focused on having enough savings for any emergency that happened, such as for unexpected medical, vehicle, or car expenses. Life's struggles and challenges have a way of appearing out of thin air, happening when you least expect it, and often can have devastating setbacks for those unprepared. As a matter of fact, according to the Motley Fool, a full third of Americans have $1,000 or less in their savings accounts[3]!

I understand that poor planning on my part does not constitute an emergency on the part of others. Therefore, I have arrived at a place of taking the time to be proactive rather than reactive, especially during difficult times, when it comes to my finances. I understand the importance of establishing a realistic budget, no matter how low my income appears. To help alleviate unnecessary stress, finances must be managed or finances will manage you.

There are a multitude of free financial resources available for you online, and through local libraries or banks, and even churches. To help get you started, I'm sharing a few steps and suggestions. The best time to start financial precautions is before you find yourself experiencing financial difficulties in the middle of a sudden crisis. However, it's not too late to take control over your money today. Managing your finances reduces stress, and provides comfort and security to know that immediate needs can be

---

[3] https://www.fool.com/the-ascent/research/average-savings-account-balance/

CHAPTER 10: FINANCES

met, while you focus on those things that cannot be delayed.

First, talk to a financial advisor or someone with above average money management skills for the purpose of helping you identify a financial plan that works for your budget. If you need help, they can also explain how to create a budget, or assist you in finding tools that do most of the work for you.

Make the commitment to establish a minimum savings of at least 10% of every paycheck you receive to tap into for life's emergencies. Identify what those emergencies are and stay firm. A car repair? Yes. A night out on the town? No. Once you get in a habit of saving, it gets much easier. As your nest egg grows, you want to see it continue to grow, and temptations to drain your savings diminish.

Surf the internet for basic information to help you gain a financial understanding of how money works, even if you do not have any savings built up yet. There's a wealth of knowledge out there, yours for the taking, and easy to find with just a quick Google search.

There is also a benefit and value in establishing a relationship with a trusted financial advisor. These individuals are trained to help those who might not fully understand the importance of financial planning. They can help you learn how to have money work for you in good and bad times. My financial advisor has helped me to create a custom plan based on a thorough assessment of my financial circumstances. This allows me to breathe easily when it comes to situations where I might need funds, and grow in a positive financial direction.

Another useful thing is to learn how to generate multiple streams of income. This is a valuable tool for anyone. By having more than one source of revenue, you are protected if something happens to one. For myself, I have improved my ability to control my income by partnering with LegalShield[4]. LegalShield provides me with an ability to protect myself, my family, and others with affordable legal protection. I honestly feel I have a legal firm at my fingertips who are dedicated to helping me make informed life decisions with more confidence than I have ever experienced. Further, when friends, family, acquaintances, and businesses partner with me in connecting with LegalShield, they each help me to keep my son's legacy alive because all earned income from LegalShield is deposited directly in my nonprofit organization's account. This makes me know that my son's death has given purpose as I strive to empower others.

Finances being managed are essential to the ability to continue living comfortably. I am pleased to share that after using these tips I am no longer overwhelmed with my finances because I have uncovered effective and efficient ways to generate funds to carry out the vision and mission of IGMA. This includes establishing healthy partnerships with individuals and organizations who can help me better understand the way money is made. I believe what I do with my money to empower others has a lasting impact. This

---

[4] You can visit this URL to learn more: BIT.LY/IGMAINC.

CHAPTER 10: FINANCES

now positions me to no longer have to beg my family, friends, and acquaintances to help me fund I Give Myself Away. William often said to me: ***"Mama, don't chase money, let money chase you."***

TURNING IN

Where am I in my thoughts today about my finances?

What did I take from this chapter as I turn in and reflect?

What have I done, or can I start doing today to begin my financial strengthening journey?

Chapter 11: Fears

Have you ever heard anyone say fear is nothing more than false evidence appearing real? Call it what you may, I realized when my son was murdered it forced me to face my greatest fear. Despite having had a dream something bad was going to happen to one of my children, I never honestly thought I would actually have to bury one of them.

Unfortunately, on that dreadful day when I received the call William had been shot, I realized it had come true, and the time to face my greatest fear was now facing me—and when I least expected it. It can be a difficult thing to face fear head on. Not all of us can do it when the fear first appears. It's also often unexpected, which can lend to the element of apprehensiveness and fright. Sometimes that not knowing really is difficult to handle. Fear can be useful, though. It can even encourage us to step outside of our comfort zones.

I recall quite some time ago praying that I might one day become a talk show host. Little did I know, my prayer would one day take flight and now serve as a reality for connecting and empowering others. Sandra (DJ Jazzy) Dunson provided me with an amazing opportunity to fulfill one of my childhood dreams. She called me at the start of 2020 and asked, "How serious are you about becoming a talk show host?"

At the time, I laughed out loud because I really thought Sandra was just making small talk. After several follow-up questions, I realized Sandra was serious about helping me

Chapter 11: Fears

to realize my dream. So I told her I wanted to be like Oprah, and even went out and purchased a children's book titled Oprah and began to read it daily to try and overcome my fear of one day actually having to pretend like I was a talk show host.

Sandra called me a few months later. "Angelia, how soon could you be ready to launch a few episodes of your talk show?"

Fear set in, and I replied, "I am no talk show host. I have never been trained. Furthermore, I am just not ready."

Sandra asked an important question. How would I know when I was ready? I told her God would tell me and let me know when He wants me to start. To my surprise, Sandra was prepared to respond with her thoughts for every one of my fears and apprehensions. She did not twist my arm or push me into anything. However, she let me know her verbal invitation was a great opportunity to realize one of my dreams, although there would be no money exchanged for being one of the first hosts on her online radio show.

So, there I was, agreeing to try my hand at this new experience amid my fears. Over the years, I've learned that I can not overcome what I did not acknowledge. It is important to build yourself up by first acknowledging the mental, spiritual, and emotional hurdles of life. More specifically, facing truths of any guilt and shame that resulted from God and bad choices. Those need to be replaced with honesty and transparency. For myself, I often looked to others to validate me because I often doubted

CHAPTER 11: FEARS

myself and my abilities to become the woman God created me to be.

Once I made up my mind to stop caring about what people thought and decided to be transparent, it propelled me further into my purpose. I stopped trying to paint over the hurts in life, instead deciding to connect with the good, bad, and ugly parts. I believe when I woke from the inside, I began to see and approach life differently.

In hopes of facing my fears, I called Belinda and shared the offer Sandra had proposed to me. I asked if she would assist in taking on the idea of a talk show as an IGMA initiative to empower others and continue carrying out our mission and vision. Although I was full of fear and not sure how to lead, Belinda said sure. I replied, "Great! Because I always wanted to be like Oprah."

To my surprise, Belinda answered, "I am only going to ride this new wave with you if you agree to not be like Oprah." Fear kicked in again. It must have been obvious, even over the phone, because Belinda quickly added, "It's not that I don't like Oprah. It's just that when she asks a question on her show, she always answers the question without giving her guest a chance to respond."

Was she right? Curious, I set out to look at past Oprah Winfrey shows, and I was able to see what Belinda meant. At this point, I became even more fearful, but I was not going to let that stop me. Fear or no fear, I stepped out on faith and accepted the challenge of becoming a radio talk show host on a fast track to leading the organization down this new path and explained how I thought we should proceed.

The thoughts in my head began to run wild because we were able to identify a host of themes we could use to operate throughout the first season, which went well considering we both were learning on the fly. After my first poor selection of song choices to nestle into each episode, a quick decision was made by Belinda to ensure all song selections would be made by her since I have no acumen when it comes to selecting appropriate songs to motivate our audience during segment breaks.

As each month passes, the fear has diminished. Because I am guilty of being an overachiever, I now view this opportunity as a challenge to be the best in my new workspace. Trust and believe, with no formal training, I often feel like giving up. However, I am determined to succeed, and every episode affords me the opportunity to keep my son's legacy alive. After many mistakes and endless days of not feeling confident about my abilities, it's good to know I am still standing, despite the inner fears and self-imposed feelings of ineptness. This fact is what makes each day and each show easier.

Today I am pleased to share, despite the huge learning curves, I have found purpose bigger than my pain. I feel like with each new episode of our show, *All That Matters*, I learn something about myself. My fears are decreasing, and my levels of confidence are continuously increasing, even to the point where others are calling in to ask if they can be on our show.

Chapter 11: Fears

Although we began this radio talk show with monthly themes for each weekly show, our second season evolved into interviews and special topics with our guest(s) each week. These incredible minds are committed to sharing great insight, resources, answers, tips, and/or strategies to help empower individuals and organizations seeking to cope or sustain. This is especially needed during times of uncertainty, and we only choose topics that matter to our listeners. These topics align with our B.L.E.N.T.H. Strategic Pillars, which are **B**usiness, **L**egal Matters, **E**ducation, **N**onprofits, **T**echnology, and or **H**ealthcare.

As our faith has grown, so has our audience. We recently were notified we will be on the TuneIn app, where over 75 million listeners can find our show. In the bonus chapter of this book, you can find out more information, including the URL to access the podcast. How blessed I feel that I pushed fear aside, moved forward with faith, and now have the ability to help others who need to be motivated, inspired, and comforted.

Fears, as I started this chapter out saying, are often false evidence appearing real. You don't need to believe those worries. You do need to trust that as you move forward, trusting in God, a way will be made for you.

"I cheated on my fears, broke up with my doubts, got engaged to my faith, and now I am marrying my dreams! Soon I will be

CHAPTER 11: FEARS

holding hands with my Destiny!"
~Eddie A. Rios

CHAPTER 11: FEARS

TURNING IN

Where am I in my thoughts today about my fears?

What did I take from this chapter as I turn in and reflect?

What have I done, or can I start doing today to begin my fear strengthening journey?

Chapter 11: Fears

Chapter 12: Lessons Learned

The 8 Essential Ingredients and my 21 Lessons Learned were birthed through years of deep meditation, a host of insecurities, gut-wrenching tears, and ever-evolving revelations. The combined list of my 8 Essential Ingredients to peace, joy, happiness, and wholeness, along with my 21 Lessons Learned helped me to overcome a feeling of complete bondage and total confinement resulting from the unexpected and senseless murder of my son. You are already familiar with my 8 Essential Ingredients: Faith, Family, Friends, Forgiveness, Food, Fiduciary Responsibility, Finance, and Fears.

There have been days when I simply felt the air has been so thick, I literally felt I could not breathe. I wanted to give up and throw in the towel on life because I was so disappointed with where I found myself after losing my son. My daily routine consisted of allowing myself to push others away so I could cope, namely because I felt I had failed my son. Often, I could see the lips of others moving as I stared into space, but I felt I could not hear anything said because I was stuck in a world of "woe is me" syndrome. Looking back, I was on a journey of self-destruction because I was confined to those thoughts of self-pity which kept me in bondage.

My journey out of confinement and bondage has resulted in a host of lessons learned. I would be remiss if I did not share these as a great place to start if you or someone you know has found themselves experiencing a pain like mine. My 21 lessons learned are in no particular order; however, each was discovered at the appropriate time for me to grow into the person I am today. Thus, I encourage you to read each of the 21 Lessons Learned and apply one, if not all, of them to help empower you (or someone you know) if you are in similar pain.

Life is a schoolhouse of continuous learning and development of self. Pain and suffering are a part of life, and which we all experience at one time or another. To progress in life, we have to see life on a daily slate of opportunities. Within each day, we are all given twenty-four hours. At the same time, the way we take up space can oftentimes determine whether we get another twenty-four hours after our day has elapsed.

In order to fully enjoy each day above the ground, we must remind ourselves each day is filled with lessons to be learned. Please understand the 21 Lessons Learned are not presented in any sequential order and nor do I have a favorite lesson. Each has importance and value.

As you read each of these, stop and take a moment to consider how you can also make this change or apply this lesson to your own experience or situation. Consider making your own list of lessons learned, as you grow and walk in faith and knowledge.

21 Lessons Learned

1. The greatest source of strength comes from knowing and keeping the presence of God nestled in my heart.
2. A piece of peace is better than no peace at all.
3. **Will P** means **W**ork, **I**nspire, **L**ive **L**ife, **P**lease!
4. Forgiveness is what we do to others for the empowerment of ourselves.
5. To hear, one must LISTEN, which requires you to be SILENT.
6. True purpose begins with individual daily praying and planning.
7. A victim mentality holds you captive and in bondage of the mind until you choose to exercise your right to be free.
8. Grief is a heartache and no one can tell you when it will end.

9. Life in and of itself is worth living for, especially when others are counting on you to shine a light to help them see their way.
10. Become a beacon of light for others.
11. Bringing awareness to invoke change in society requires commitment and support from others.
12. Relaxing requires one to let go and let God order your steps.
13. In a journal, list the blessings of God to remind yourself He hears and answers prayers.
14. Encouraging others when you are going through your own struggle inspires the person you are trying to encourage, in addition to positively inspiring yourself.
15. It is okay to remember, commemorate, and celebrate the living and those who have departed.
16. Confinement is not all bad if you return healthier and whole from the roller coaster ride.

17. Loving yourself starts and ends with self-care. Tell yourself, I am no longer a victim because I am victorious!

18. Striving to G.R.O.W. means to set long and short-term GOALS, RECOGNIZE your realities, OBSERVE your options (obstacles and opportunities), and WIN with Christ Jesus!

19. Demonstrating care is confirmation and self-approval.

20. Never stop serving others, as the best compliments are those we never hear.

21. Identifying and repeating a favorite quote daily is a great recipe for healing.

At the start and the end of each day, I wholeheartedly believe *Turning In Is the Only Way Out*. As you move forward in your own journey of healing and discovery, remember that the experience requires understanding of who you are as a person and what you need to feel whole again. It is my humble desire that something you read in these pages will help you through your journey.

CHAPTER 12: LESSONS LEARNED

"Knowledge is only information, as the real power is in the application of knowledge."

CHAPTER 12: LESSONS LEARNED

TURNING IN

What are my lessons learned?

What did I take from this chapter as I turn in and reflect?

What have I done, or can I start doing today to begin documenting my lessons learned?

Chapter 12: Lessons Learned

THE RESULT

WHAT WAS THE RESULT OF OUR LETTERS TO THE COURT TO BLOCK WILLIAM'S MURDERER'S PAROLE?

William's shooter is currently serving the remaining twelve years of her twenty-year prison sentence. Sadly, this is the maximum number of years one can serve for manslaughter in Alabama, as the court system does not offer different degrees of murder according to the Alabama Law.

Bonus Chapter

This bonus chapter is where you'll find more detail about some of the things I'd mentioned in my book. You'll find URLs, addresses, specific names and mentions, as well as a few other things that I felt were important, but I didn't want to interrupt the story to share.

Connect with Me

I'd love to talk with you, hear your story, and connect. You can find out more by visiting:

www.goshenpublishers.com/dr-angelia-griffin

Places

The funeral service for William Paul, II was held Thursday, December 9, 2010 at 2:00 p.m. at Destiny World Church located at 7400 Factory Shoals Road, Austell, Georgia under the leadership of our Senior Pastor Wilbur T. Purvis, III. My older brother Prophet Marlon Griffin delivered a very uplifting sermon.

BONUS CHAPTER

MUSIC

I'd mentioned in Chapter 2, a list of song titles based on the Psalms that were helpful and healing for me to listen to. While this is not an all-inclusive list, several favorites were:

- "He Has His Hands on You" by Marvin Sapp (Psalms 91)
- "As I will Bless the Lord at All Times" by Byron Cage (Psalm 34)
- "O Give Thanks Unto Our God" by Fred Hammond (Psalm 118)
- "The Lord is My Shepherd I Shall Not Want by The Brooklyn Tabernacle Choir (Psalm 23)
- "The Lord Is My Light and My Salvation" by Andrae Crouch (Psalm 27)
- "O Praise the Lord For He Is Good" by Lighthouse Assembly of Believers (Psalm 107)
- "Lord Teach Me That I May Know" by The Psalms Project (Psalm 143)
- "I Will Bless the Lord at All Times" by Byron Cage (Psalm 1, 2, 3, 4)
- "How Majestic Is Your Name" by United Voices Choir with Anthony Brown (Psalm 8)

BONUS CHAPTER

FAMILY

Incredibly important to me is that my family members know how much I appreciate each of them. While I'm sure I've missed a few names, and that is my own fault, not the lack of another, I wanted to take a moment to thank these specific individuals more deeply for their support.

Rather than name each individual, I hope I do not offend anyone simply because I have elected to reserve this portion of this book for the names of a few key people who have been a major part of my family support squad. I often feel my family is an extension of me, and although there are a host of people on my priority list of family members, I decided to publicly share a grief gratitude list. On this list, I named the people I called my immediate family supporters. I am extremely grateful to each of them.

The names on my list include my mother, Fannie Griffin, whom I am extremely grateful for her motherly guidance, strength, prayers, and never-ending encouraging words. My brothers, Prophet Marlon Dewayne Griffin and Charlie B. Griffin, for unwavering love and support from the day of Will's death until this present day.

Prophet Dewayne used his amazing ability at my son's homegoing service to present scriptures supporting Will's life from A through Z. He was also very instrumental in helping lay the foundation for our nonprofit organization to remind us William is "Gone, but he shall never be forgotten".

> BONUS CHAPTER

Charlie B. Griffin is my younger brother, and I am very proud of the difference he continues to make in our ever-evolving local community. I humbly appreciate his continued willingness to allow me to lean on and draw from his ability to shine, despite life's hurdles. My brothers and I are so different, yet alike, in our understanding of our respective purpose to serve others and make lemonade when life hands us lemons.

My amazing daughter Star, "my mini me" has so much more confidence, charisma, and style, and I am thankful for her maturity I have witnessed firsthand. My daughter and I have had many conversations regarding the loss of her brother and best friend.

Another I have leaned on and for whom I am grateful for is my daughter-in-love, Keta, who religiously strives to keep Will's legacy alive. Keta is more than my daughter-in-love, she's big sister to Star, mom to my grandson Khalil, and a dear friend to me. Like Star's letter, Keta's letter to the Pardons and Paroles Board left me in tears and signaled the level of maturity that has since helped me beyond words.

Through all my seasons of reflections, my one and only grandson has been the reason I have continued to gain strength in overcoming the devastating loss of my son. When he said, "Grandma, you have got to stop all of this crying. You know my daddy is not dead, he is just sleeping with Jesus!", from that day on, my tears began to diminish.

The rest of my family, including nieces, nephews, aunts, uncles, cousins and their extended families, have continued to undergird me in ways I never knew I needed from each of them. I am forever grateful to each of them.

Friends

Friends often turn into family. How blessed I am to have the love and support of so many I can call my true friends. I'd like to further mention these individuals for their extended support.

While I appreciate all the people whose paths I've crossed over the years, especially during the days leading up to and after the death of my son, I would be remiss if I did not name a few of my true friends. I sincerely appreciate my longtime schoolmates, lifetime godparents, and aunts of my children: Belinda and Linda.

Also, I'd like to acknowledge the following, my spiritual mentor Mary P. Ford and mentee goddaughter Shelbra. Destiny World Church (DWC) in Austell, Georgia and Pastor Wilbur T. Purvis III. DWC ministry leaders Barbara Phelps and Elder Sharon Turner. Photographer Mel Burton. Professional mentor and educational colleagues Dr. Samuel Sanders and Dr. Philip Neely Jr, along with peer mentor and colleagues Dr. Mary Ann Hughes-Butts and Bobby Hart. Longtime aunts of my children, Chandra Cheeseborough-Guise, Karen Jones-Morene, Margaret Smoake, and Yolanda Ward Williams. My loving sisters of Delta Sigma Theta, especially my DST sisters of the Marietta Roswell Chapter, sorors at other amazing Delta chapters throughout the

United States, and my awesome godsent angel, Attorney Azzie Taylor.

All That Matters Radio Show

The weekly radio talk show is Saturday evenings from 5 pm to 6 pm EST. You can listen along at: **www.artistic-throttle.com/index-radio.html**

After each radio broadcast has aired, the audio only recording is posted on our I Give Myself Away, Inc Website (www.igmainc.org/podcast) for replay at 9:00 p (EST) the evening after the show airs.

Look for *All That Matters*, also on the TuneIn app.

Appendices

The following pages contain information regarding how to establish a nonprofit organization should you desire to start a nonprofit in memory of your loved one.

Additionally, I have included letters sent to the Alabama Pardons and Parole Board to petition the denial of parole for the woman who murdered my son.

These letters may be helpful for you if you need to craft your own, but also allow you to see a different perspective as it pertains to the court case.

APPENDIX 1

How to start a 501c3 nonprofit organization

For a complete fill in application to obtain a 501c3 nonprofit organization – public benefit please visit: Church on the Road.

www.churchontheroad.com

Be sure and tell them Dr. A. referred you and receive a 20% discount.

TEXT: IGMA FREE CONSULT to 334-552-1119 to schedule a complimentary 15-minute call with Dr. Paul to answer questions and help you start your nonprofit.

APPENDIX 2

Your Tax-Donations are always welcomed and appreciated at:

https://www.igmainc.org/ a 501c3 Public & Charitable (tax-deductible) nonprofit organization.

WILLIAM DONALD PAUL II "STOP THE VIOLENCE" ENDOWMENT SCHOLARSHIP

https://www.igmainc.org/

For more information, please contact 770-422-4048

I Give Myself Away

https://www.youtube.com/watch?v=Ha3JbND1Sqg

www.igmainc.org

APPENDIX 3

CAMPAIGN LETTERS TO DENY PAROLE

June 1, 2021

State of Alabama
Bureau Of Pardons and Parole
100 Capitol Commerce Blvd, Suite 310
Montgomery, AL 36117

Dear Alabama Bureau of Pardons and Paroles
ATTN: Board Operations Representatives

Writing this letter to you today makes me feel as though I must defend the value of my son's life all over again to ensure the bad behavior of [Perpetrator: KAJ] is not lost in your decision to uphold the law. Thus, on December 2, 2010, the evolving life of my amazing, loving, and intelligent son William Donald Paul II was unnecessarily ended at the selfish hands of the senseless murderer: [Perpetrator: KAJ].

My heart hurt then and hurts even more with each passing day since December 2, 2010, when I learned [Perpetrator: KAJ] had murdered my son. Presently, I watch my grandson grow up without his loving father, my daughter strives with much difficulty trying to carry on her life without her big brother and best friend. My 83-year-old mother shares often how much she misses her kind-hearted first grandchild (Lil Bill). His dad communicates with me frequently, how much he misses Williams' wisdom. His godparents, aunts, and uncles alike remind me often, especially on his birthday and his death day, how bright William was and how much they miss his wisdom.

Sad but true, not a Mother's Day goes by that my voicemail and social media are not flooded with RIP wishes and calls to share how much William is missed and the difference he has made in the lives of others. At all our family functions we talk about how William was the glue that connected all his cousins over the years. Today, all we have are pictures and fond memories of my son and a common denominator that we all sincerely miss William Donald Paul II and wish that fatal day when [Perpetrator: KAJ] unnecessarily pulled the trigger and ended his life had never happened. We agree the only justice is knowing [Perpetrator: KAJ] is behind bars and does not get the opportunity to commit another senseless crime for 20 years.

When I look back over the past ten years, I recall two significant turning points in my life. First, the day when my son William Donald Paul II decided to re-enroll at Alabama State University (ASU) in August of 2010 at which time he decided to live off campus as a mature and proud upcoming junior at ASU. Second, less than five months after I personally moved my mission-minded son into his apartment, I learned he tried to stop two off campus young women from fighting, at which time I received the call and

APPENDIX 3

was told William had been shot and he lived long enough to identify as the person who shot him!!

Initially I experienced major denial and pain as only a mother could because I felt an inability to protect my child who was on a path to greatness. Weeks later, I was advised by the judge, we would be going to a grand jury to hear this senseless case. I recall walking out of the courtroom with a heavy heart and tears streaming down my face, at which time I approached [Perpetrator: KAJ] and I told her to her face "**I forgive you!**" I heard [Perpetrator: KAJ] tell her attorney when he asked, "who was that" and she replied, "I think that was his mom"! At the time of sentencing, I distinctly recall Judge Hardwick stating because she had not shown any remorse throughout the entire trial, he would deny her parole when the time came for any consideration of parole.

Fast forwarding to now having served less than eight years behind bars of a 20-year sentence for manslaughter in which [Perpetrator: KAJ] admitted killing my son, I view her behavior then and now as senseless bad behavior with no respect for human life when she violently and brutally pulled the trigger several times aiming her gun at my son. Thus, I wholeheartedly maintain the bad behavior warrants the need to keep her behind bars and **NOT** be released before the completion of her 20-year sentence.

For the record, the prosecution proved beyond a reasonable doubt that [Perpetrator: KAJ] did not act in self-defense. She is an adult bully and she demonstrated reckless behavior when she murdered my son. Her reckless behavior resulted in a 20-year sentence consequence. Thus, I recommend **only after completing her 20-year sentence** should she be mainstreamed back into society. The thought of any consideration of parole for [Perpetrator: KAJ] and the serious nature of her offense in murdering my son undermines respect for the law and sends a negative message to anyone who chooses to senselessly take the life of another person.

In closing, this correspondence is sent to your attention because we have arrived at the point where a decision must be made **to PLEASE DENY PAROLE of** [Perpetrator: KAJ]. In other words, I am humbly requesting [Perpetrator: KAJ] REMAIN behind BARS for her entire 20-year sentence for the senseless murder of my son William Donald Paul II. Yes, I forgave her for killing my son William, however, I CANNOT forget her selfish senseless actions!!!! At the very least, [Perpetrator: KAJ], a federal prisoner committed a senseless crime; therefore, she must complete the time for the crime without any opportunity for parole. Stopping the violence begins with holding the people who commit senseless crimes accountable and ensuring parole is not granted!!!!!

Humble Respect,
Dr. Angelia Griffin

"I cheated on my fears, broke up with my doubts, got engaged to my faith, and now I am marrying my dreams!

APPENDIX 3

Soon I will be holding hands with my Destiny!"

~Eddie A. Rios

Appendix 3

Confirmation Letter from the Alabama Pardons and Parole Bureau June 2021

ALABAMA BUREAU OF
PARDONS & PAROLES
100 CAPITOL COMMERCE BOULEVARD MONTGOMERY, AL 36117
PAROLES.ALABAMA.GOV | 334.242.8700

KAY IVEY
GOVERNOR

CAM WARD
DIRECTOR

June 16, 2021

Dr. Angelia Michelle Griffin
Jacksonville, Florida
Via email: Dr.a1231@gmail.com

Re: Kandi Adina Johnson
AIS # 284161

Date of hearing: July 21, 2021

Dear Dr. Griffin:

Thank you for your letter of June 1, 2021. Your letter has been prominently flagged as a protest to parole and has been made a permanent part of Johnson's file.

I can assure you that your feelings and comments will be before the Board when a decision is made in this case.

Sincerely,

Ashley Harbin
Victim Services Director

APPENDIX 3

To Whom This Opposition Concerns

Today, I am humbly writing on behalf of my late brother William Donald Paul II who was murdered by [Perpetrator: KAJ] on 12/2/2010 two days after my 20th birthday. William was my older brother, first friend, first protector, first supporter, confidante and so much more. As I sit here and write this letter holding back tears still in disbelief that my brother is no longer here due to [Perpetrator: KAJ]'s senseless actions that still carries a significant pain and void in my heart that will never be filled.

When we were informed that [Perpetrator: KAJ] was up for parole, it felt like the nightmare started all over again from getting the phone call that my brother had been shot and countless years we had to sit in a courtroom watching [Perpetrator: KAJ] lack remorse. [Perpetrator: KAJ] has made it crystal clear she is not sorry for her actions which she even stated nonchalantly while in court 2012 "that she guesses she was sorry for taking my brother's life." As she shrugged her shoulders I will never understand how could a mother of six be so cold-hearted and ill mannered.

Furthermore, [Perpetrator: KAJ]'s parole should be denied at all costs. [Perpetrator: KAJ] is clearly a menace to society, just review her track record. At the end of the day, [Perpetrator: KAJ] played God and took the life of a vibrant, non-violent, very much-so loved individual, a brother, son, friend, classmate, and last but not least a father. His son Khalil Paul is now fourteen; he was four when his father was violently and abruptly taken from him. Do you know how heart-rendering it was to explain to my nephew that he would not be able to have his daily car rides with Daddy anymore? That all the bonding activities Khalil had grown accustomed to are no longer possible and just hold onto all the memories they shared. I am forever thankful for the moments my brother and his son shared; however, no child should have to grow up without a parent. To know that [Perpetrator: KAJ] is still able to see her family since she's stationed in Alabama is utterly not fair. [Perpetrator: KAJ]'s family is still able to talk to her, see her, and establish new memories even though she has done the despicable.

With all that being said, I often question is she even truly being punished? Yes, she is confined in a space; however, she is still living her life with no remorse for the unjustifiable pain she has caused to my family. I pray this opposition is reviewed with a clear heart and mind of someone with the understanding for what is right and what is wrong. Please, I beg of you to do the right thing and not grant her parole, and may she remain in prison to fulfill her entire sentence. With all due respect, who knows what she is capable of since she obliviously does not fear the law.

Thanks for reviewing my opposition
Star Paul

APPENDIX 3

June 6, 2021
State of Alabama
Bureau Of Pardons and Parole
100 Capitol Commerce Blvd, Suite 310 Montgomery, AL 36117
Dear Alabama Bureau of Pardons & Paroles ATTN: Board Operations Representatives
Re: [Perpetrator: KAJ]
Please deny parole

I knew this day would come, but I didn't imagine the feelings that would overcome me when I opened the email informing me of [Perpetrator: KAJ]'s impending parole hearing. My godson, William Donald Paul II, was murdered at the hands of [Perpetrator: KAJ] on December 2, 2010, the day before my 50th birthday. When I addressed the court at her sentencing I stated then, if I live to be a hundred years old, I will not and cannot forget that day. Well, here we are 10 years, 6 months, and 4 days later and I am now 60 years old. I have not forgotten. I also stated at that hearing that I wished I could say that 20 years was enough.

Today I feel like someone has ripped the stitches from a healing wound. My heart is heavy. As a praying woman, I prayed this morning as I did the morning of [Perpetrator: KAJ]'s sentencing. I asked God, as I did then, for his infinite wisdom and guidance in writing this letter. It is ironic that the same two words that God gave me then have been placed on my heart today, "Compassion and Remorse". Two things that I didn't see from [Perpetrator: KAJ] in the course of not one, but two trials. In my obedience I am not going to take this time to demonize [Perpetrator: KAJ]; her actions spoke loud and clear, and have continued to echo over the years. You see, death is only final for the deceased. The rest of us have to carry on and live with the consequences of our actions, and in this case, the consequences of the actions of others. I am attaching with this letter a letter that I have kept in my Bible for the past 10 years. It is relevant because I'm certain that throughout the course of these proceedings you are going to hear a lot about [Perpetrator: KAJ], and how much she has changed. I need you to know who Bill Donald Paul II was.

Bill's godfather and I were asked to write this letter of recommendation for Bill (William Donald Paul II) in February 2008 when Bill was considering joining the armed forces. A decision that I was both proud and apprehensive about. He ultimately decided on attending Alabama State University instead. A place where he could grow and excel. Never could I have imagined that the war that would take his life would be steps from his front door. Now I ask myself "What if"? You see, for those of us left to grieve, this question is a constant. What if [Perpetrator: KAJ] was the person on December 2, 2010 that she wants you to believe she is today. I will never know. Bill's family and friends will never know. Bill's son will never know. What I do know is that my heart sinks every time I think of this one question his son asked. "What did my daddy do that was so bad that lady", [Perpetrator: KAJ], "had to kill him." We will never know.

Bill's sentence was death. [Perpetrator: KAJ]'s sentence is 20 years. "So be the scales of justice."

APPENDIX 3

As always, walking in faith,
Belinda Carrington

July 16, 2021
Alabama Bureau of Pardons & Paroles ATTN: Victim Services
100 Capitol Commerce Boulevard, Suite 310
Montgomery, AL 36117
To the Parole Board:

    I made it to the scene on that cold night in December and wasn't fully prepared for what I was about to witness. The worst memory of that day wasn't seeing William's lifeless body lying on the cold pavement or hearing those dreadful screams from his friends and loved ones. I'll always remember the words that came out of [Perpetrator: KAJ]'s child's mouth, which he said with much enthusiasm, "My mama just shot a n***a." I could only stare in disbelief; as I could only imagine the environment that child must've been subjected to. To know that those are the values and teachings that [Perpetrator: KAJ] instills in those individuals whom she raised is truly disgusting. I wholeheartedly believe her children and the rest of the world are better off with her remaining right where she is – behind bars.

    My son is now 14 years old and he has spent the last 10.5 years of his life reliving memories of his dad through photos and shared stories from families and friends. However, that alone is not enough to stop the hurt and constant questioning of what life would be like if only his dad was still here. To this day, I've invested countless hours and resources in victim support groups and grief counseling services for my child, all to no avail – the hurt and grief still lingers. While we appreciate everyone's love and support, that will never stop the hurt or fill the empty void caused by the careless actions displayed on Dec 02, 2010 by [Perpetrator: KAJ].

Due to her senseless behavior, William Paul lost out on many of life's most precious moments shared between a father and son. He wasn't able to teach our son how to ride his first bike, how to tie his first tie, and most recently, watch him graduate from middle school.

My child carries the burden of knowing that he'll start his first year of high school without his dad, his dad will never be in the stands at any of his games, won't be there at his future graduations, and will never be there to witness his wedding day.

[Perpetrator: KAJ] showed a true depiction of her character on December 2nd, 2010. From the smirk on her face in her mugshot to the nonchalant demeanor displayed in the courtroom during sentencing – she's shown that she just simply doesn't care and has no remorse. It is my hope that the courts continue to set an example for all individuals such as [Perpetrator: KAJ] who display no remorse for their despicable actions; never taking into account how their actions affect the lives of so many others.

Ultimately, I hope that the board is able to hear our cries through these letters, and deny the parole of [Perpetrator: KAJ]. She deserves to serve the duration of her sentence behind bars; as she is a danger to her family, society, and quite frankly anyone who happens to be in her path - if she's simply having a day. We need to set examples for our youth and show them that there are consequences for every

APPENDIX 3

action; and also instill trust and faith in the American justice system. Thank you for your time and consideration.

Mother/Guardian of Khalil A. Paul (Deceased Victim's Son)

Made in the USA
Columbia, SC
22 March 2022